# Masters at Work

MASTERS AT WORK

# BECOMING A CURATOR

HOLLY BRUBACH

**SIMON & SCHUSTER**

*New York   London   Toronto   Sydney   New Delhi*

Simon & Schuster
1230 Avenue of the Americas
New York, NY 10020

First Simon & Schuster hardcover edition September 2019

SIMON & SCHUSTER and colophon are registered trademarks of Simon & Schuster, Inc.

For information about special discounts for bulk purchases, please contact Simon & Schuster Special Sales at 1-866-506-1949 or business@simonandschuster.com.

The Simon & Schuster Speakers Bureau can bring authors to your live event. For more information or to book an event, contact the Simon & Schuster Speakers Bureau at 1-866-248-3049 or visit our website at www.simonspeakers.com.

Manufactured in the United States of America

1   3   5   7   9   10   8   6   4   2

Library of Congress Cataloging-in-Publication Data has been applied for.

ISBN 978-1-9821-2684-1
ISBN 978-1-9821-2685-8 (ebook)

FOR DAVE MASTERSON,

IN MEMORIAM

# CONTENTS

"Warm. Sunny. Curated. That's your Caribbean," says Silversea's ad for its cruises. Gwyneth Paltrow, in partnership with J.Crew, modeled "eight outfits curated from the fall collection." A *New York Times* comedy critic recommends a weekly Brooklyn stand-up show as "superbly curated." Curating, an activity once confined to museums and galleries and carried out by trained professionals, has become the favorite pastime of every influencer with an Instagram account.

Initially, curating entailed bringing an educated eye to bear on art, wielding the impeccable taste and discernment that comes with long exposure to masterworks. The halo of expertise persists though curating in the popular sense requires no credentials. Any shopper with a sense of style can become a self-appointed curator whose authority is ratified by a legion of followers. At which point curating confers value: the books Oprah chooses rise to the top of Amazon's frequently purchased list; the makeup beauty bloggers promote sells out at Sephora.

So ubiquitous is this exercise of assessing the world and ranking everything in it that it's easy to lose sight of the fact that there are people—still—who work as curators in the traditional sense of the word. Many are based in museums and galleries. Others, independent, direct big exhibitions, often on an international scale, like the Venice Biennale or Documenta in Kassel, Germany. There are curators who act as advisers to individuals and corporations, helping them assemble and maintain a collection. There are curators who steer artists' estates, positioning their legacy, ensuring that the work is taken care of and seen in a sympathetic context, placing it with museums and determining what to sell.

If your interest in curating is in becoming a tastemaker and building an empire on sponsored posts, this is not the book for you. If, on the other hand, you're curious about what happens when you train your mind's eye on art and bring that art to the attention of the public, you're in the right place. This book explores the curatorial profession through the life and work of one of its leading practitioners.

Meet Elisabeth Sussman. Her title since 2004—the Sondra Gilman Curator of Photography at the Whitney Museum of American Art—doesn't begin to convey the breadth of her expertise or the responsibilities of her job. Over four decades, at museums in Boston, San Francisco, and New York, Sussman has passionately championed artists across multiple disciplines. As a result, their work has become more widely known and highly regarded. You may recognize one or more of their names: Diane Arbus, Eva Hesse, Florine Stettheimer, Robert Gober, Paul Thek, Mike Kelley, Gordon Matta-Clark, Nan Goldin . . . The list goes on. But unless you work in the art world or read reviews of museum shows, chances are you've never heard of Sussman. Which is, to her mind, the way it ought to be.

There are rock-star curators as famous as the artists they show, who post photos of their celebrity friends on their Instagram pages. Sussman has no Instagram page. Like many if not most curators like her, she prefers to go unannounced.

"It's always about the artist," says Adam Weinberg, the Whitney's director and Sussman's boss. "It's not the Elisabeth Sussman show, putting her name in lights."

David Ross, former director of the Whitney and the

San Francisco Museum of Modern Art, for whom Sussman worked in both places, says, "Elisabeth's not in it for the fancy friends and the social prestige. She's worked a long and complicated career, she's done things that are intellectually and critically significant, and she's never compromised. She's the real deal."

Lynn Zelevansky, a curator herself, former director of the Carnegie Museum of Art in Pittsburgh, and Sussman's collaborator on major shows, says that curatorial work requires a unique combination of skills. "It's very creative. You need to be a scholar—maybe you learn that in graduate school. And then you need to know how to interpret someone's story in space and over time; some of that you might get through on-the-job training. But I think there's a certain degree of talent, too. It's not super common to get all those qualities together in one curator. Elisabeth's got the whole thing." Zelevansky considers Sussman an excellent representative of their field. "She's sort of the best that we can do."

Tony Ganz, a Los Angeles–based film executive who loaned works from his collection for Sussman's retrospectives of Eva Hesse, Gordon Matta-Clark, and Paul Thek, says, "Elisabeth is in a league of her own in every way. I think people are probably disarmed by her warm, affable presence. But just under the waterline is someone who will look for the truth where other people will just accept clichés, and that will lead her to an understanding of these artists she gets so involved with and committed to that other people might miss."

Diminutive, dressed in black, her dark hair cut short, blue glasses framing her eyes, Sussman has the appearance of a scholarly pixie. On a Friday night in November 2018, she attends a dinner hosted by David Zwirner, the New York art dealer, at his house in the East Village. The occasion is the opening of *Untitled*, sixty-six photographs from Diane Arbus's last project. Arbus died in 1971, before she could finish editing the negatives. Doon Arbus, the photographer's daughter, to whom the task of managing her estate fell, has now made a definitive selection of the images that this show comprises, some of them on view for the first time. The evening also marks the start of a partnership between the Fraenkel Gallery, a highly regarded San Francisco showcase for photography, and Zwirner, with galleries in New York, London, and Hong Kong. Together they will represent the estate worldwide.

In this company, Sussman is known for her landmark 2003 retrospective *Diane Arbus Revelations* at the San Francisco Museum of Modern Art. For that show, in collaboration with Doon, Sussman assembled postcards, letters, notes, and other records of the photographer's thoughts that offered a deeper understanding of Arbus as an artist and as a person.

Going to gallery openings is part of Sussman's job. This evening has more heft than most, if only because the artist has been dead for forty-seven years and because the project she considered the culmination of all her years of work has at last been presented whole. Both Doon and her younger sister Amy are in attendance. The forty guests have been drawn from the art world A-list. At a table in the far corner, opposite a wall dominated by a huge Cy Twombly, Sussman is seated between Jeffrey Fraenkel, founder of the San Francisco gallery that bears his name, and Robert Gober, a New York artist with whom she has worked since early in both their careers.

The conversation turns to lighting. David Chipperfield, the English architect whom the Metropolitan Museum of Art has commissioned to design its new wing, talks about the stringent policies museums have lately adopted in an abundance—some would say overabundance—of caution, reducing light in the interest of conservation. Sussman recalls working with one photographer, Zoe Leonard, who wanted her work seen in brighter-than-usual light and prioritized the installation—a decision that ran counter to the standard protocol of showing the most beautiful print with the most interesting provenance, which can only be seen under restricted light for a restricted period of time. Instead, Leonard made a dedicated set of "exhibition prints" explicitly for the duration of the show.

But that was a onetime solution for a single show. In many museum galleries, the lights have been dimmed, making it harder to experience the art in all its nuances and details. The table's consensus is that this is a shame and that it's the monetization of art that is largely to blame. As prices for contemporary art have climbed, those who show it are increasingly playing it safe for fear that too much light will harm the art and reduce its value. The stakes are higher than ever—so high that prices have gone beyond the reach of most public institutions, which changes the calculus in terms of which art ends up where. "Museums today can't afford to buy the art they show," Sussman laments.

"The artists and photographers working when she started—there was no market," Fraenkel says a few days later. And that made for a certain freedom, which was "both a minus and a plus." Take Arbus, for example: a single mother struggling to support her kids, hoping to make a living through her photography. "The magazines were the only thing that paid," Fraenkel continues. "Nobody was going to buy the pictures. Now aspiring photographers have exhibits in high school, and by the time they go to art school, they've already thought about their gallery trajectory." Fraenkel calls this careerist landscape "a curse young artists today are born into. Elisabeth fell in love with art before that."

For all her success and recognition, Sussman represents only one kind of curator at a time when there are many. Others who work in big museums may spend their lives not curating exhibitions but thinking about the collection and tending works of art, specializing in a particular period, like nineteenth-century French painting or the Italian Renaissance or Modernism. And these responsibilities vary from one museum to the next. "In the contemporary art museum in particular," says Scott Rothkopf, chief curator at the Whitney, "we have maybe a different idea of what being a curator means in terms of being an advocate for artists and trying to make sense of the time that we're living in."

"There are different models," notes Jane Panetta, an associate curator at the Whitney, in charge of the museum's 2019 Biennial, who has looked to Sussman's example and sought her out for advice. "There's the big personality who's maybe great with boards, very external facing, with broad-brush visionary capabilities and the ability to excite people about an idea; that's one model." Curators of that variety often go on to become directors. And then there's a different model, "maybe not heading toward a director position, and that's more Elisabeth. It helps that she's been an appealing, passionate, compassionate, funny, thoughtful person along the way. But more important is the fact that she's been open-minded and hardworking and brilliant, and that's why she's where she is. It's not because she's been super-charismatic." Sussman isn't naïve enough to think that star power and bold ideas don't matter, but, Panetta says, "she's also made a commitment that she's not going to traffic in all that stuff. She's just going to be about the work."

When Fraenkel calls Sussman "old-school," he means it as a compliment. "She has a quality surprisingly rare among curators," he says. "She actually loves the art. I cannot think of an exhibition she's done that has lacked a depth of feeling."

To hear Sussman talk, you'd think that curating was some kind of highbrow service industry. Which, in a sense, it is. Something gets triggered when the art finds its way into her mind. "There are little doors that can open up through your senses," she says. "That's where it starts"—in reaction to breathtaking beauty or some aspect of the work that "gets to" her in some other fashion. Through those doors lies "something you hadn't thought about, some road to enlightenment. With the artists I've worked on, all I'm doing is allowing myself access to a certain kind of joy through what they've found, in their brilliant ways. And then, through me, the public has access, too."

# 2

I f you set out to invent the ideal curator, it would be hard to come up with a childhood better suited to the job than Sussman's.

Born Elisabeth Sacks in 1939 in Baltimore, she was the first of four children; two brothers and a sister followed. Her mother, a painter, was the only child of Hungarian Jewish parents, whom Sussman calls "very interesting." How so? "Not because they had done anything distinguished," she explains, "but just because they didn't fit into American life." (Make a note of this: her career-long fascination with misfits dates all the way back to her own grandparents.)

Her mother attended the Maryland Institute, a respected local college of art, while her father, a musician, from a family that owned a food store, enrolled at Peabody Institute, a renowned local conservatory, to continue his violin lessons. When Sussman speaks of her parents' adolescent years and early twenties, it's with evident admiration for the discipline and commitment they brought to mastering the technique their respective art forms required.

But the likelihood of their earning a living by those means, much less supporting a family, seemed slim. So her parents changed course: her father attended medical school at the University of Maryland and became a hematologist; her mother trained as a librarian at a large Baltimore library and eventually took a job at a private school. "She was very proud of having a profession," Sussman recalls.

Her mother continued to paint. Her father continued to play the violin. There was always music at home. Elisabeth was sent to studio art classes taught by a painter in space rented from Claribel and Etta Cone, the Baltimore sisters who had befriended Gertrude and Leo Stein, traveled to Europe, and amassed a vast collection of paintings and sculptures by Picasso, van Gogh, Cézanne, Gauguin, and Matisse, plus Middle Eastern textiles, African sculpture, Indian metalwork, and Japanese prints. (Their astonishing collection, donated to the Baltimore Museum of Art upon Etta's death in 1949, now resides in a dedicated wing containing more than three thousand works.) "When I think about the early brushes that I had with art other than my mother's work," Sussman says, "it was the environment of going to this art class. To leave and then walk down through the Cone sisters' apartment was just staggering. So it's funny to think that now I work at a museum."

Sussman was also sent to the Peabody Institute for lessons in Dalcroze eurhythmics and, later, to classes with a former dancer who lived next door—one of the Isadorables, the troupe of six girls Isadora Duncan had chosen, trained, and later adopted. Sussman's parents took her to see the ballet companies that came to town.

In 1951, the family commissioned a young architect by the name of Paul Richard Schubert, who was working in the studio of a local modernist named Alexander Smith Cochran, to design and build them a home. The result was "a very radical house for Baltimore," Sussman says—a glass box with a flat roof, set in a clearing surrounded by trees. A fireplace and bookshelves divided the living and dining areas.

Long-playing records had recently been introduced, and her father had become obsessed with high fidelity, installing sophisticated equipment and creating the optimal acoustics for listening to music. The glass box of a house, open to the slanting rays of the sun, reverberating with Bach cantatas and Mahler symphonies, was filled with books, including Modern Library editions of the classics.

Sussman's recollections depict a charmed life in a mid-century Eden that enshrined creative endeavors of all kinds. It was the manifestation of a persistent ideal that found expression in the modernist conviction that culture exerts a civilizing influence on human nature.

And then her father died. He was fifty-five. Though not unexpected—he'd received a terminal diagnosis several years before—his death left her bereft.

Having finished high school early, Elisabeth had gone off to Earlham College, a Quaker liberal arts school in Indiana, where she majored in the humanities; and then after two years she transferred to Simmons College, a women's school in Boston. There she met a Harvard graduate student by the name of Herbert Sussman, who was getting his PhD in nineteenth-century English literature. They married in 1960, when she was twenty-one, "I think to fill the great, gaping hole my father was about to leave behind," she says.

Because she loved books, she'd vaguely assumed that she, too, would go to graduate school for English and pursue "something literary" without quite knowing what that might be. "But I chickened out," Sussman recalls. "My mother was convinced that the only way I could be literary was to do what she had done, which was to become a librarian." Simmons had a program for that. "And by the time you finished, you would have learned to be something. So that's what I did."

Although Sussman describes herself as "a dutiful daughter," her mother, she says, was shaken by her marriage to a future teacher of literature; despite all the early exposure to art and ideas, this was not the life her mother had in mind for her eldest child. "I think somewhere in my parents' ideal sense of us," Sussman says, "my mother would have been happy if we'd gotten big houses in Baltimore and gone swimming in the social scene that they had laid the way for." The conventions were slow to change. "There were two kinds of women in those days. Some were very capable and drove cars and earned money, and some didn't." Although her mother was one of the capable ones, she could just as easily have been a housewife. "The house and the way it looked—all that was very important to her. The problem is that she really wanted to be both."

Many daughters are steered, either overtly or subliminally, onto the path their mothers were obliged to forgo. Sussman, however, found her own way without challenging her mother's status as the artist in the family. "I always had this sense that I was going to be an intellectual of some sort in the arts," she says, "rather than an artist myself."

Touring galleries with her, I repeatedly found myself wondering how Sussman viewed her mother's paintings. What were they like? "In a style a little bit like Ben Shahn is how I think she would like it to be described," she says. "Very precise, a light touch. City scenes, landscapes." It's typical of her to see the art from the point of view of the person who made it—in this case her own mother. While most of us, encountering a work of art for the first time, give it a scant few minutes to make an impression, Sussman devotes her full attention and as much time as it takes to understand what the artist intended. Her reservoir of sympathy is far deeper than the average viewer's. With a perpetually open mind, she approaches the art and starts every conversation with the artist from a place of respect. In an era when most viewers are impatient, distracted, pressed for time, and prone to snap judgments, she consistently meets the art on its own terms.

ON A FRIDAY AFTERNOON in December in New York, as the gray daylight fades, Sussman and I drop by the Alexander and Bonin gallery in TriBeCa, which is showing paintings by Stefan Kürten, a German artist. Neither of us is familiar with his work. As we study a series depicting what appear to be mid-century modern houses in a setting that looks like generic Palm Springs—with swimming pools, glass walls, tropical vegetation, and a lone metal Bertoia chair casting its diamond-patterned shadow on a concrete terrace—Ted Bonin, one of the gallery's partners, provides background commentary: the artist, who lives in Düsseldorf, is a guitarist as well as a painter; he begins a new work by covering the canvas with a layer of gold paint before building the images, which results, even after overpainting with color, in a kind of sun-drenched glow. Recognizable as the houses would seem to be in their details, they exist only in the artist's imagination. One interior features a Jackson Pollock painting on the wall and an oriental rug on the floor, with the labyrinthine drips and motifs fastidiously rendered.

Sussman crosses the room to get a closer look at *Perfect World*, a large, intricately patterned canvas that, from afar, appears to be a scrollwork of honeylocust branches. Up close, it becomes clear that many of the leaves are letters forming words—EUROPE, DEATH, COCAINE, HATE, COCA-COLA, WORLD BANK, GREED, LIES, FAMILY, CNN, EVIL, SILENCE, LSD,

HITLER—interspersed with symbols for recycling and yin/yang, the Christian cross and Star of David, euro and dollar signs, the BMW, Chanel, and Google logos. There is no judgment—not yet. Sussman files all this—the ideas, the images—away in the vault of her memory. Her mind cross-references the information, finding affinities and connecting ideas, so that the mammoth backlog of the art she's seen helps make sense of each new work she encounters.

## 3

Even if it had occurred to Sussman in college to aspire to the career she ended up having, as a curator, there was no road map for doing so at the time. The field was evolving, and Sussman herself would become part of that evolution. She made up her career as she went along, charting a course that, however unprecedented, in retrospect appears inevitable. She has invented not only her own role in the art world but also, in large part, the role of a curator of contemporary art as we now understand it, for the benefit of those who have come after her.

After earning a degree in library science at Simmons, then working at a suburban library outside Boston, Sussman made up her mind that she wanted to study art history: "It was my time and my money, and there was no mother or father telling me whether I could or not, so I just started." Her first course, through the Harvard extension program, was in baroque architecture, taught by a remarkable professor named Henry Armand Millon, who held degrees in English, physics, architecture, and the history of art. That course, she says, "completely blew my mind."

The study of art history, the traditional training ground for museum curators, stopped in those days with Cubism and Surrealism, if it got even that far. Contemporary art was regarded with skepticism: a work's quality would only become apparent with time, when it assumed its place in a canon that took shape years later. Every so often a living artist like Picasso or Matisse evinced such outsized talent that there could be no doubt he would be written into history, like mid-career baseball players destined for the Hall of Fame. But otherwise the moment, when you were in it, could cloud your judgment. Only hindsight would enable the experts to make sense of the present.

"If you went into art history in the mid- to late sixties, it was all about these Germans who had come here to teach," Sussman recalls. The focus was on connoisseurship, distinguishing the real from the fake, authenticating works by Italian Renaissance painters or Old Masters. "If you wanted to learn about contemporary art, no one was going to teach you, because they didn't know. You had to go look at it yourself." So she began frequenting galleries, looking at art. In

Boston, the Harcus Krakow Gallery in particular was catering to a new breed of collectors, and the art on view was in keeping with the work being shown in New York.

After two years, Herb got a job teaching at Berkeley; they moved in 1963. "It was very dramatic to travel that far away from my big, overbearing family," Sussman says. "Life for me had developed up and down the Eastern Seaboard. But off I went, kicking and screaming.

"Don't ask me why, but I thought I would get a degree. I'd found a program at Boston University that would take me in, and when we moved, I sort of took it with me in a suitcase." BU allowed her to complete her studies at Berkeley, where she enrolled in more courses. "To say I went to graduate school is kind of an exaggeration," she says. "I did end up getting an MA, but it was on the run." Degree in hand, she thought, "Okay, wonderful. I paid for it. I wanted it, and it turned out to be something I was interested in. Now what?"

FOR THE FIRST HALF of the twentieth century, it was the galleries that showcased the work of living artists—as they still do today. Museums like New York's Metropolitan

Museum of Art, Europe's national coffers like the British Museum and the Louvre, and smaller institutions around the U.S. were regarded, and regarded themselves, as repositories of cultural artifacts. Their curators were stewards, putting artifacts on display, ensuring their safe transfer to the next generation. But as it happened, three museums born in the 1930s, all within the bounds of Manhattan, took on contemporary art as their crusade. To reflect his own enthusiasm for early abstraction, Solomon R. Guggenheim established the Museum of Non-Objective Painting under the guidance of a woman artist, Hilla von Rebay. The Museum of Modern Art, steered by its first director, Alfred Barr, mounted small accessible exhibitions of current artists. The Whitney Museum of American Art, founded in 1931 by Gertrude Vanderbilt Whitney, an artist herself with a distinguished personal collection, operated according to a different model: as a kind of artists' club, offering support in the form of classes and, on occasion, medical expenses or trips abroad. The Whitney's Annual and Biennial exhibitions became important showcases for artists at various stages in their careers.

Under Barr's auspices, Dorothy C. Miller, curator of MoMA's department of painting and sculpture, organized a series of six exhibitions over twenty-one years, beginning in 1942, titled simply *Americans* and either the number of artists in the show (e.g., *15 Americans*) or the year (*Americans 1963*). Each, in Miller's description, was "a group of small one-man shows" featuring the work of living artists. Although MoMA had been founded by three women—Miss Lillie P. Bliss, Mrs. Cornelius J. Sullivan, and Mrs. John D. Rockefeller—it was very much Barr's preserve. In the thirty-four years Miller worked there, she "developed no power base of her own," according to a survey of her exhibitions by Lynn Zelevansky; "hers was largely a reflected light."

Sussman says she was dimly aware of what Miller had done, but not to the extent that she looked to her example as a model for her own career. The circumstances seemed unique to that period and its cast of personalities at MoMA. There was still no job titled "Curator of Contemporary Art," just a handful of curators and museum directors who happened to know some artists and shared the conviction that people should be exposed to the art being produced in their own time. In California, a man named Walter Hopps opened an adventurous gallery in Los Angeles and went on to direct the Pasadena Art Museum (now the Norton Simon Museum of Art), where he gave Kurt Schwitters, Joseph

Cornell, and Marcel Duchamp their first retrospectives. His career would later take him to Washington, D.C., and eventually Houston, where he participated in the founding and early years of the Menil Collection. Hopps is today regarded as one of the first curators in America to have built a career on the work of living artists. But much of that was still to come during the years Sussman and her husband were living in California.

Mostly they were trying to keep track of what was going on right there in their own front yard. Berkeley had become a hotbed of political radicalism and the burgeoning counterculture, a scene Sussman describes as "just nuts and fabulous at the same time." Tom Freudenheim, one of Herb's childhood friends, had come to town to direct the Berkeley Art Museum. "He and Leslie, his wife, had this great, glamorous life," Sussman says. "They were going out all the time, getting dressed up, meeting interesting artists, stuff like that. I got involved, and that drew me away from all the shenanigans I'd been a part of: everybody was taking sides, getting teargassed. But then, suddenly, there was this other idea, that maybe a life working in a museum could be amazing and interesting and fun."

She and Leslie cooked up a project: they would write a

guidebook to the residential architecture of Bernard May-beck, who worked primarily in Northern California and de-signed numerous local houses in the American Craftsman style. "This was at a time when nobody was interested in the Arts and Crafts movement," Sussman says. But, with Herb's focus on nineteenth-century literature, they'd made trips to England, where they saw a lot of William Morris's designs, and she recognized the connections between his work and Maybeck's. What started out as a guidebook turned into a scholarly undertaking as she and Leslie gathered an enor-mous quantity of information. *Building with Nature: Roots of the San Francisco Bay Region Tradition* was published in 1974, and the book's photos, by Ambur Hiken, became a travel-ing exhibition, picked up by the Smithsonian. "That was my first experience of museums," Sussman says. "So suddenly here I was with my foot in the door."

Then her life rearranged itself again. Herb was denied tenure at Berkeley. By this time they had two children—Charlotte, born in 1965, and Lucas four years later. They moved the family back to Cambridge, because that was where they wanted to live, and Herb took a job at North-eastern University.

Not long after they arrived, Sussman met Jonathan Leo

Fairbanks, whom she describes as "a very progressive guy," then curator of the American decorative arts department at the Museum of Fine Arts in Boston. Fairbanks specialized in American architecture, furniture, and crafts. "Oh, we've got interests in common," he told her, on the basis of her book about Maybeck. "Why don't you come and work for me?" It was the last place Sussman expected to end up, with its collection built around Thomas Chippendale and Paul Revere. But she agreed, starting out part-time on a volunteer basis. Her first assignment, as preparation for a show Fairbanks wanted to do, was to track down all the H. H. Richardson furniture in Boston: church pews, library tables, and chairs. Eventually she began to be paid.

And then, as the American bicentennial approached, she was brought on staff. Fairbanks had landed an enormous grant from Philip Morris for an exhibition about the American West—"I guess because they had the Marlboro Man, and it was all being handled by their very flashy PR firm," Sussman recalls. "They had great ambitions for this, including an international tour." Although Fairbanks's name was on the show, he was occupied with any number of other responsibilities, so Sussman found herself overseeing it.

In the end, the idea proved to be more compelling and

offbeat than cowboys and the usual scenic painters who celebrated the desert landscape. She and Fairbanks built the exhibition around the notion of the Western frontier and what it represented: the scientific exploration, the displacement of large numbers of people, the interface with Native American populations. Fairbanks was particularly interested in furniture and what it looked like in, say, mid-nineteenth-century Santa Fe. So they consulted the small-town historical societies and found genuine artifacts, including sketchbooks, journals, and ledgers. Sussman took on charting the frontier in photography done for the building of the railroads. "They had a whole professional team," she recalls, including the designer of all the MFA's books, the registrars who took care of the loans. "They told me what to do." The show was titled *Frontier America*, and because it coincided with the American Bicentennial, it traveled to six cities, including Europe. Sussman traveled with it, overseeing the installation in each new venue.

It had been a big undertaking for a small institution, an all-hands-on-deck situation that proved to be wonderful training. By the time it ended, Sussman knew every technical aspect of curating a museum show. "Everybody who has a position like mine can tell you a story like that," she says. "You can't learn how to do the job in school."

The money was good and the experience was great, but becoming a permanent member of the MFA's department of American decorative arts was not Sussman's goal. She decided to take a break to spend more time with her children. Meanwhile, Fairbanks had been part of a graduate program in American studies that had grown up at Boston University. "And it became a really solid and fascinating department," Sussman notes, "because American studies can include film or art or literature or whatever." It was one of the first hybrid degrees, and this particular program had alliances with museums so that students could benefit from internships, some of them at the MFA. Having worked there, Sussman was already familiar with the program and the people involved. "So I decided I would do that," she says. "I liked being a student. I guess at that point I was still thinking, 'Should I finish and get a PhD in art history?' I decided I would do the PhD in American studies."

Among her teachers in the program was William Curtis, an Englishman younger than Sussman at the time, who taught the history of American art. His deep interest in Jackson Pollock and the Abstract Expressionists was exciting, and his seminars made her reevaluate her plans. Ultimately, she took her exams in art history and passed. Then she had to settle on a topic for her dissertation. While she hemmed and hawed, the head of the American studies program arranged an internship for her at the Institute of Contemporary Art in Boston. The internship, when it was done, turned into a job offer.

She took it because the first project was so compelling. Isabelle Storey, who was on the staff at the ICA at the time, was putting together *Homage to Walker Evans*, a show of work by the pioneering photographer, her second husband, who had recently died, and she asked Sussman to work on it with her. "At that point, I had died and gone to heaven," Sussman recalls, "because Isabelle could tell me stories, all kinds of stories, about Evans." That clinched her decision about the future. She went back to her art history advisers and told them that she wouldn't be getting her PhD because she'd gotten a job instead—a job that she liked.

This was 1976, and the ICA was small, a function of its minor standing in a city widely regarded as a backwater when it came to modern and contemporary art—a view that the small staff had tried repeatedly to change, to no avail.

After a series of rapid administrative changes, including the departures of Storey, who was Sussman's boss, and Gabriella De Ferrari, the director, Sussman found herself making up half of the remaining curatorial staff. She mounted an exhibition of the work of Florine Stettheimer, the American painter, poet, set designer, and *salonnière*, who had died in 1944. (Some fifteen years later, Sussman would follow up with a second Stettheimer show, at the Whitney.) After the hiring of one new director, whose tenure proved to be short-lived, another search turned up three candidates, including Thomas Krens, who came with ambitious plans for expansion. (He would later take the Guggenheim global.) The board asked her, "as the survivor of the ship," as she says, to weigh in. She strongly backed David Ross, who had been at the Berkeley Art Museum. "He was full of interesting ideas—not about real estate but about programming, how to make the ICA relevant and responsive to what was going on artistically." Ross got the job.

David Joselit, now a Distinguished Professor of Art History at the Graduate Center, at the City University of New York, was then a Harvard undergraduate with hopes of becoming a curator and critic; he was already writing art reviews for the *Boston Ledger*. He sent Sussman a letter. She invited him to work with her as her intern on a show called *Art and Dance*, which was already in the planning stages.

"The thing that was so extraordinary about Elisabeth then is that she was so ambitious. Not career-wise; that's not what motivates her. She was ambitious about projects. She does these projects that shouldn't be possible, like that show. She figures out how to make something work in a gallery that shouldn't work in a gallery."

The exhibition, which David Ross describes as "completely unheralded," featured a Matisse costume, drawings by Bronislava Nijinska, Isamu Noguchi sculpture, and live performance by Douglas Dunn. When Joselit finished his undergraduate degree, he joined the ICA in 1983 as an assistant curator and worked with Sussman for another six years.

Massachusetts at the time was governed by Michael Dukakis and his wife, Kitty. In his long-range strategy for propelling himself to higher office—in 1988 he would run for president as the Democratic nominee, losing to George H. W. Bush—he was intent on changing the state's profile from the home of the Puritans to a nexus of new ideas. The Massachusetts Council on the Arts and Humanities dispensed "what seemed like gobs of money" to the ICA, Sussman says. Then the Rockefeller Foundation came on board with travel and research opportunities. Add to that the contacts Ross brought from all over the world, and suddenly the ICA went from a boutique operation to a major force in what was happening in art.

Joselit calls the ICA in their time "a scrappy institution with very little infrastructure. We had difficulties keeping the lights on, and then we would get these grants to do these ambitious shows, punching above our weight."

Marian Goodman, who had founded a New York gallery in her own name in 1977 and would go on to become one of the most highly respected and powerful dealers in the art world, had a major client she would visit in Boston, where she and Sussman met. Sussman calls Goodman "the person who kicked me into consciousness. I remember her telling me as a young curator, 'You've just got to travel. Show up. Go to Europe and see what's going on.'" Sussman and Joselit made frequent trips to New York to see the work on view in the galleries and get to know artists.

"David Joselit and I decided we would try to make something coherent about what we were doing," Sussman says. "So we came up with two significant theme shows." The first, which caught the attention of the New York art world, was *Endgame*. This was in 1986, and it presented artists who came to be regarded as the signature talents of the eighties—Jeff Koons, Philip Taaffe, Sherrie Levine, Peter

Halley, and Ross Bleckner—organized around ideas about the end of painting and art becoming a commodity.

Sussman and Joselit also wanted to publish what they were doing, to create some lasting record. She suggested that they commission critics, historians, and theorists—among them, Yve-Alain Bois and Hal Foster. "We said to all our prospective authors, 'We can't offer you much money. But it would be really good if you could come to some studios with us as we meet and talk to these artists. You don't have to like what we're showing, and you don't have to support what they do in what you write.'" MIT Press agreed to pick up the catalogs, which have since become collector's items.

Among the young New York artists who interested her was Robert Gober. She had seen his sculptures of sinks at the Paula Cooper Gallery and set up a meeting to offer him a show at the ICA, which was slowly acquiring a sterling reputation in the art world. "The great thing about being outside New York," Joselit says, "is when you do something that isn't good, they don't notice; but when you do something good, they do."

Gober was familiar with what she and Joselit had been doing. "More than the New York institutions," he says, "the ICA had its finger on the pulse."

———

GOBER AND SUSSMAN AND I are revisiting the start of their relationship. In the Chelsea building that now serves as his studio, we sit in the back of the ground floor, behind the garage, while an assistant works nearby. A balding man with salt-and-pepper stubble and lively eyes behind glasses with a thin wire frame, Gober comes across as someone who misses nothing. His two dogs, Hoohoo, a rescued Catahoula, and Bean, a harrier hound, come and go.

Sussman selects the artists she works with carefully, and her interest in their work in many instances becomes a commitment that outlasts the duration of the show. Her relationship with Gober, spanning multiple projects over three decades, has the tenor of a lifelong conversation: warm, candid, and thoughtful, with an undertone of wry humor and a baseline of mutual respect.

"I mean, this was 1985," Sussman recalls. "There I was, working for a pittance in a museum that nobody paid any attention to. And you weren't dying to be in shows—or were you? Were you dying to be in shows at that point?"

"Probably," Gober replies. "I was ambitious, yeah."

"But you didn't have that aura about you," Sussman continues. She went to his studio, which was then in Little Italy. "And I told him I wanted to show his work with another artist I had in mind; I had some cockamamie idea about why they would look good together. And Bob flat-out said he didn't want to be part of it." She was undaunted by his refusal. "Bob had this somewhat independent practice by then," she explains. "He'd done two shows combining his work with the work of other artists. Which," she says, turning to face him, "you orchestrated."

"Yeah, I wouldn't call it curating," he replies. "But it arose out of being put in group shows and my surprise at how uninteresting or obvious the couplings were. So I thought, 'Well, do it yourself.'" He would invite artists to show with him, then convince a gallery to present them. The first of these—"the one that absolutely blew me away," Sussman says—took place at Nature Morte, a small, conceptually oriented gallery run by two artists in a narrow East Village storefront. Sussman remembers "pieces of fractured furniture and exquisite light."

"It was a headboard of a bed, and a chair," Gober says. There were two sinks on the wall. "These things were together in this very mysterious setting," Sussman interjects, "and they had a profound effect on me."

Cable Gallery, which gave many prominent artists their first shows, had hosted a subsequent installation—"a little more ambitious," according to Gober—in which he combined his own work with that of three other artists, including Meg Webster, who made sculptures out of earth. That, too, had made an impression on Sussman: "So I said, 'Okay, let's do it your way.'" There was no brainstorming. "I knew I was in good hands. I totally handed over the reins."

*Utopia Post Utopia: Configurations of Nature and Culture in Recent Sculpture and Photography* opened at the ICA in January 1988. The space, Gober later noted in a chronology of his work, was "unfortunate." In response, he built a room within it. The existing wall-to-wall carpet was stripped to expose the original cement floor, which turned out to be different colors because it had been poured at different times. The inside walls were painted robin's-egg blue, with white baseboards and molding that Gober made by hand; the outside remained unfinished, like the back of a stage set. The spectator entered through a doorway. Inside was the door, off the hinges, painted white, propped against one wall; hanging on another, Albert Bierstadt's 1867 painting of Lake Tahoe, California; a handwritten joke by Richard Prince, framed, on the third; and, freestanding, a bed Meg

Webster had made out of dirt and covered in moss, which grew during the show.

I recall seeing one of Gober's early shows—a configuration of sinks on the wall of a gallery—and being moved by it, but I could not have told you why. They reminded me of sinks I had seen at my grandmother's house or in janitor's closets or at salvage warehouses, utterly plain but beautiful in their unabashed utility, torn out to make way for newer, fancier models. Marcel Duchamp came to mind, and the urinal he had famously appropriated—an outrageous gesture that set art in the twentieth century on its course. Now here was Gober, some seven decades later, with an object he might likewise have purchased but chose to construct instead, as if to appreciate its form in painstaking detail and preserve the essence of it.

Sussman, in her catalog essay, recaps Gober's prior installations and the ideas that emerged from them, including the chair and headboard from Nature Morte, "signs of the now lost everyday world of the recent past," she writes. "The space is rendered archaeological." She traces the emotional impact to the elements he brings into play: "Decay, memory (of an American domestic past), sleep, recuperation—activities at once physical and psychological—as suggested by objects both found and created . . ." Like Marianne Moore's real toads in imaginary gardens, Gober's subject matter, Sussman says, finds its form in "literal things" in "imagined rooms."

Writing about visual art—or any art that's nonverbal—can be problematic, requiring both precision and a poetic use of language. We rely on an expert to take apart our experience of a painting, a symphony, a ballet, without reducing the work to mere mechanics. Sussman doesn't shy away from this responsibility, and she manages to leave the mystery intact. "Something's always going to have a material presence that you have to explain," she says. "It's going to have a complex of ideas that the artist brings to it that you can share. That's my job, because I've been privy to the artist, and I've spent time with the materiality of the thing, getting it into a gallery, on a wall, lit properly. So I've thought about the way it's made. And then I have to explain to people what I think the artist intended and help them not to be afraid of it, to find a way into it. My Bob Gober may not be your Bob Gober. I'm trying to arrive at some sort of shared sense of what the artist's work means, but it might be unstable. I'm completely at home with that."

TOWARD THE END OF the eighties, Sussman and Joselit were asked to work together, along with Trevor Fairbrother, then curator of contemporary art at the Boston Museum of Fine Arts, on the "Binational," an exhibition of contemporary American artists assembled parallel to an exhibition of contemporary German artists mounted by two museums in Düsseldorf, after which the two cities would swap shows. They asked Gober to participate; also Mike Kelley, a performance artist from Los Angeles who had begun to incorporate environments and objects that shared ostensibly linked subjects.

Kelley's installations, Sussman remembers, "had very convoluted stories. It was like nothing I was in any way ready to understand, but there was something intrinsically, fabulously interesting about all these concocted stories and ideas he was working through. I couldn't get it to begin with. But he could talk me through it, and then I could get it all. I loved the wit and the genius and the complexity."

She offered Kelley a solo show—his first—at the ICA and secured an NEA grant to underwrite it.

In 1989, in the midst of a firestorm over public funding for the arts, the Corcoran Gallery of Art in Washington, D.C., canceled its exhibition of over 150 photos by Robert Mapplethorpe, who had died of AIDS a few months earlier. The content—blatantly homoerotic, occasionally violent—was deemed too incendiary to put on display within walking distance of Congress. As planned, the show traveled to the ICA in Boston, where it proved no less controversial. David Ross was interviewed repeatedly on television, defending the show and the rights of artists. He and Sussman had had a good, steady run at the ICA, going on a decade, and he was ready to take a break; the board had granted him a sabbatical. But the Whitney, which had weathered opposition to its own Mapplethorpe show a year earlier, needed a new director, and the search committee offered him the job. He took it and took Sussman with him. The ICA had given her the latitude to develop her skills, expand on her ideas, collaborate with artists and scholars she admired, exercise her point of view, and develop her voice. The Whitney would amplify it, placing her on the front lines of the raging debates at the heart of the culture.

**4**

Working with artists, planning and creating exhibitions, orchestrating the installation in the galleries, drafting the accompanying text, writing and editing the catalog—all this is what you might expect a curator like Sussman to do, but she estimates that it's only 50 percent of her job, and that's even higher than it might be for other curators who aren't so focused on exhibitions, whose positions entail full-time oversight of permanent collections or other aspects of museum operations. Included in this half of how she spends her time are reading, going to galleries, and paying visits to artists' studios. Anyone who works in contemporary art at a major museum, she says, expects to do a lot of general "R & D"—research and development— "because that's what you're hired to do, to keep up with the scene and be a little bit ahead, if possible."

Other duties include overseeing department budgets and various aspects of museum administration, and, depending on the institution, more public-facing responsibilities like speaking at events intended to broaden the audience or cultivate relationships with board members. "I know curators who are basically also travel planners and social directors," Jeffrey Fraenkel says. "There's nothing wrong with that, although in an ideal world, this would have nothing to do with the job. But it's not the ideal world we're living in." He concedes that certain museum trustees find these skills valuable.

"Being a good fundraiser is very helpful," Scott Rothkopf adds. "And also, I think, understanding the market, if you're a curator involved in building a collection. A lot of curators don't want to think about the market, I think because that feels sort of tawdry or separate from the issues that they came into the field to pursue. But if you're responsible for spending a limited budget, no matter how big it is, you ought to have a clue as to what a sensible expenditure is. That's part of being responsible to the institution."

Curatorial studies programs like the one at Bard College, in Annandale-on-Hudson, New York, can provide training, Rothkopf says, but the students he meets coming out of them are mostly interested in curating group exhibitions around particular themes or ideas—a model epitomized by curators like Harald Szeemann, a Swiss curator who died in 2005, and Hals-Ulrich Obrist. The curator begins with an argument and finds the artists whose work supports it—a method that is in many ways the antithesis of Sussman's approach, which starts with the art or the evidence and allows the ideas to emerge from it. The notion of doing a retrospective on a single artist is "almost old-fashioned" as far as these students are concerned, Rothkopf claims. "It's not something they study because, I think, the assumption is that that sort of show curates itself. You take a bunch of things and you put them in order, or the artist does it." Though the majority of Sussman's most successful shows have been monographs, it would be hard to argue that they've curated themselves—so deft is the guiding hand behind them, leading us time and again to the intersection of the artists' work and their inner experience in ways that mere chronology can't deliver.

At the Whitney, as at many other museums, as you make your way up the corporate ladder, the nature of the job shifts dramatically, however similar the titles may sound. In ascending order: Curatorial Assistant (Kelly Long, Sussman's assistant), an entry-level position; Assistant Curator (Elisabeth Sherman, Sussman's former assistant, though promotion to this level is by no means assured; Associate Curator (Jane Panetta, in charge of the 2019 Whitney Biennial); Curator (Sussman); Chief Curator (Rothkopf); until finally you reach the office of the Director (Weinberg).

The path to the top in museums often goes through the curatorial department, though that hasn't always been the case. Just as in book and magazine publishing, where it's frequently an editor who becomes the publisher, in museums some curators move on to administrative positions with bigger titles and higher salaries. In both cases, the chance to run the company is a promotion and the logical next step in an upward career path. But just as there are editors-turned-publishers who have suddenly found themselves once removed from the text and realized that it was the close collaboration with authors and manuscripts that they found most gratifying, there are curators who accept the offer to run a museum, only to discover that what they love doing is working with artists and mounting shows. Like many museum executives, Rothkopf misses the firsthand engagement with the art. "What is ninety percent of Elisabeth's job is now only ten or twenty percent of mine," he says.

A museum director's responsibilities—courting donors, refereeing competing agendas, managing the fiscal health of a nonprofit institution—require skills not usually part of a curator's standard tool kit, which is more geared toward studying, paying attention to a single subject for extended periods, and formulating ideas over time. "Everything that makes curators great also makes them bad directors," says Elizabeth Easton, director of the Center for Curatorial Leadership in New York. A curator herself and former chair of the Brooklyn Museum's department of European painting and sculpture, Easton cofounded (with Agnes Gund) the Center for Curatorial Leadership in 2007, in response to the fact that museums were filling their highest positions with business managers, and curators who wanted to be considered for the jobs weren't even getting interviewed. "I thought you could more easily teach business to the art people than art to the business people," she says.

In the old days, a skeleton staff might consist of the director, the curator, and the conservator. But then the administrative contingent started to grow, adding staff for development, education, marketing—initially to relieve the curator from having to take on these additional burdens. "And the whole administrative part got so huge," Easton continues, "that eventually it deprivileged the curator," limiting his or her access to the director. "Curators felt that they had a lot of responsibility and very little authority."

Only working curators are admitted to the program, to which they devote four weeks over five months, taking courses that include Change Management, Managing Up, Negotiation, Finance, Managerial Accounting, and Conflict Management, taught by Columbia Business School faculty. The final week is a residency, in which they spend every day, "from breakfast to dinner," Easton says, with the director of a museum not their own. She takes pride in the fact that of just over one hundred graduates to date, 87 percent received a promotion; many have become department heads. In only a decade, the program has already produced thirty directors.

Sussman has had the good fortune throughout her career to work for directors who have understood that curating is a creative endeavor. Rothkopf, her current boss, has recently been appointed Deputy Director, which, in addition to his responsibilities as Chief Curator, entails "taking off my curator hat and sitting around the table managing finances and thinking about the fundamental viability of this institution," he says. "Most curators are not thinking in such great depth about budgets and money, and in a way, speaking on behalf of those who work for me, I think that's good. I would like to think about those things so that they don't have to. Not in a way that's patronizing, but in a way that hopefully gives them the freedom to be creative and interested and do the best work they can do."

As museums have adopted the tools of corporate metrics for quantifying success, becoming increasingly focused on attendance, or the "gate," the kinds of shows that are Sussman's specialty are becoming endangered. "The art world has been slowly sinking into show business over the last twenty years," Ross says, "and it's now ruled by the same demographics and box-office metrics, so you can show your corporate sponsor that you're bringing in the eighteen- to twenty-five-year-olds with purchasing power and that attendance is better than it was at this time last year.

"Elisabeth's shows," he continues, "were never the shows that I would hope would help balance my budget within any particular year. But that was my job." Ross tried to time exhibitions in such a way that they would balance one another out in terms of box-office appeal. When in 1992 the Whitney mounted an Agnes Martin show—prestigious and important but destined for a limited audience—it also did a Jean-Michel Basquiat show, to bring in the crowds. "I was paid a lot more money than my curators," Ross says, "to take on the grief of fundraising and play the corporate CEO role. I tried to prevent them from having to engage in anything more than the work necessary to do great shows and publish great books."

When Ross left the ICA, Sussman served as Acting Director while the board looked for his replacement. They interviewed her for the job—one of only two times in her career that she has contemplated the transition from curator to director. In both instances, she thought better of it. "I like what I do," she explains. "The money is probably the only thing that would've attracted me. But I want to be on this side of what goes on in a museum, and there are many things about administration that don't interest me. The power in itself has no attraction." No one who knows Sussman well tried to change her mind. The consensus among her friends and colleagues is that she was born to do what she'd been doing, not supervise other people doing it.

"I remember at one curatorial meeting," Rothkopf says, "we were talking about the advancement of women as museum directors. Elisabeth of course supports that. But she spoke very passionately about her role as a curator and not wanting to be seen as a kind of underachiever because she hadn't gone on to be a chief curator or a museum director." For Sussman, curating is not a stepping-stone to anything; it's a choice she has made and an end in itself.

# 5

Over a decade at the Institute of Contemporary Art, Sussman's shows consistently garnered respect in New York, but the reviews in Boston were unanimously negative. You might think the chorus of critical disapproval would have immunized her against the sting of bad press. But as it turned out, nothing could have prepared her for the tsunami of loathing that greeted her first big undertaking at the Whitney, the 1993 Biennial.

The museum's commitment to show the work of living artists dated back to Gertrude Vanderbilt Whitney herself, who inaugurated the tradition in 1932, one year after the museum opened, with what was then intended to be an annual exhibition. Other shows at the time, based on the European model, relied on juries to decide which artists to include, which works would be put on display, and which of those were deserving of prizes. Instead, the Whitney invited the artists directly, and the artists decided what to show. The reviews claimed that the museum's good intentions made for a mediocre exhibition.

It became the show that everyone loved to hate. Every few years, according to the critics, it reached a new low. In 1937 the Whitney accelerated the pace, mounting two surveys—one for painting in the fall and another for sculpture in the spring—until 1959, when it reverted to an annual schedule, with painting and sculpture alternating years.

By the late 1960s the Biennial came under fire for admitting too broad an array of artists. Critics called for curators to narrow the field. In 1969, John I. H. Baur, the museum's director, allowed that it was no longer possible to "approximate a cross section of the creative trends of the moment." Curators began to build the shows around chosen themes. In 1973 the frequency changed to every two years. That way, Bauer joked, "you only get clobbered every other year."

Robert Hughes, the critic for *Time* magazine, called the 1985 Biennial, with its concentration of East Village artists, the "worst in living memory." The next show was met with a parallel exhibition by the Guerrilla Girls, an activist group of feminist artists protesting the Biennial's low percentage of women and minorities. That was also the year that marked a consolidation in the art world: one-third of the artists included in the Biennial were represented by four galleries that dominated the market. The 1991 Biennial, with its themes of race, sexuality, and AIDS, was regarded as provocative and even confrontational.

Sussman knew to expect some controversy. "All the neo-Expressionist painting that started up in the eighties was dead," she says. "It was over. We were onto something entirely different. The Whitney had been criticized: everybody said, 'They're eating out of the blue-chip galleries' hands.' I knew the museum was under fire. And I thought, 'Okay, that's not what this show is going to be about.'"

Although she insists she's not "strategic" in her approach to curating a show, deciding what she's after before she goes out looking, on this occasion she made an exception. It was paramount that the Biennial address the issues she sensed were running like an underground stream beneath the culture at that moment—issues that had to do with diversifying the world we live in and the art we look at. Sussman wanted to drill down and find those currents. "I thought, 'Gee, there are a lot of people who have never been in this museum before.'"

She assembled and led an all-star team of three fellow Whitney curators: John Hanhardt, head of the museum's film and video department; Lisa Phillips, who had organized thematic exhibitions and important retrospectives of mid-career artists (in 1999, she was appointed director of the New Museum); and Thelma Golden, a former curatorial assistant at the Whitney who'd left for a job at the Studio Museum in Harlem (which she now directs) and returned to run the Whitney at Philip Morris, the museum's midtown showcase for installations by emerging artists. An African American from Queens, Golden was then six years out of Smith College, brilliant and ambitious, with a point of view that Sussman lacked: "I was very aware of the fact that I'd never worked with somebody who wasn't white." Here was the chance. "Choosing Thelma to work with me, I knew where I wanted it to go—where I felt Biennials hadn't been," she says.

"The environment Elisabeth created was open and deeply respectful of different voices," Golden says. "That was one of my first experiences working on a curatorial team, and in many ways it became a model for me. Elisabeth was at once a member of the team and its leader. She led from the center, not the front."

Being a recent transplant and not long in the job, Sussman was unfamiliar with the protocol. Dealers would take her to lunch; it was only later that she realized they were lobbying her to include their artists. She and her team for-mulated their own ideas as they conducted a search for new talent that hadn't yet been filtered by the market, going out of their way to track down women and people of color.

Those who subscribe to the widespread notion of the cu-rator as gatekeeper, with the power to make or break an un-known artist's career, regard casting a Biennial as an obvious opportunity for bestowing or withholding visibility. For a young artist, the stakes can be high. There are stories of the lengths people have gone to just to get their faces in front of curators scouting for candidates, staging seemingly casual encounters on the street.

"I find the whole issue of power very uncomfortable," Sussman says. "I mean, I'm sure I have it—but I don't feel it." She shifts in her chair. "I mean, of course it's true," she continues, "but it's not a way of operating. Mostly, I think people who are in power and who like it, who are aware of it, are the people I least want to know."

FOR THE FIRST TIME in the history of the Biennial, white male artists were in the minority. There were more instal-lations and mixed-media works than paintings. It was as if the doors to an exclusive club had been flung open. Many of the artists refused to confine themselves to the formal concerns that had set the parameters for the better part of the twentieth century. Much of the work seemed intent on making a point: Byron Kim's abstract grid of eight-by-ten-inch panels, each painted to match an individual's skin color; Janine Antoni's masticated lard and chocolate, made into lipsticks; Glenn Ligon's *Notes in the Margin of the Black Book*, with reproductions from Robert Mapplethorpe's photos of black men juxtaposed with framed texts, taken from sources as disparate as Jesse Helms and the poet Ntozake Shange, as commentary on gayness and blackness; Gober's stacks of newspapers, bound as if for recycling, with front-page stories for a world where the headlines reflected more humane priorities and the ads called into question consumers' dreams. In one room, George Holliday's video of the Rodney King beating played on a continuous loop. This was Sussman's idea. "It seemed to me so relevant, the fact that it was so vivid in our minds. It was like the Zapruder film. I wanted to embed the video in the show rather than just run it in the theater."

Visitors, when they paid at the door, received tin badges as proof of admission, printed with words that, all together, formed a statement: "I CAN'T" "IMAGINE" "EVER WANTING" "TO BE" "WHITE." This, too, was a work of art, conceived by Daniel J. Martinez as a performance in which visitors unknowingly participated, figuring out the full sentence by reading other people's tags.

"It was an amazing time to be making a show," David Ross recalls. The 1992 election marked the end of the Reagan-Bush years and the start of the Clinton era. There was, Ross says, "a remarkable sea change in American culture—a lot of pent-up anger and frustration, and also a certain hope. It was a complicated moment."

In the catalog essays, some members of the team felt compelled to proactively acknowledge the complaints soon to come their way. "Many may call this Biennial the

'multicultural' or 'politically correct' Biennial," Golden ac-
knowledged. Ross, in his introduction, exposed the fallacy
underlying the most predictable line of attack, as if to dis-
arm the horde of outraged critics on the horizon: "Oddly,
consideration of the construction of identity, central to an
understanding of contemporary society, may seem to some
inappropriate as the framing reference to introduce an exhibition surveying the past two years of American art.
Inappropriate because the issues of self and community seem
to these critics solely political, fully outside the realm of art.
Not merely outside art's territory, but beyond art's reach."

A few days after the 1993 Biennial opened, a thoughtful
review by Roberta Smith ran in *The New York Times*. She
called the show "pious, often arid" and "less about the art
of our time than about the times themselves." Nonetheless
she clearly understood and to some degree even admired
the show's objectives, commending Sussman and her team
for "breaking the biennial mold." It was, she conceded, "a
watershed." Calling the show "committed, provocative and
informative," she urged readers to go see it, "as its flaws and
achievements will be debated for some time."

Then came a second *Times* review, by Michael Kimmelman, the paper's senior art critic. The Biennial, he wrote,

"has brought various New York critics of usually discordant opinions into rare harmony; at the least, they dislike it. I hate the show." He took umbrage at its "high moral ground," which he found condescending. He complained that there wasn't enough painting and that the art provided "zero visual pleasure." In closing: "To see this sort of work in a gallery is one thing; to see it in the biennial touted as a kind of standard bearer of the era is more than most of this work can bear. It's certainly more than I could bear."

That was bad enough but, as it turned out, only the beginning. In the ensuing furor, the critics piled on, each bringing his own reasons for slamming the show. Pleasure—or the dearth of it—was one recurring theme, which Hilton Kramer cited, in *The New York Observer*. As if it were art's job to endear itself to the viewer, Peter Schjeldahl, in *The Village Voice*, decried the "indifference in so much of the work on view to whether I or anyone else likes it or not." "A fiesta of whining," Robert Hughes proclaimed in *Time* magazine, "preachy and political." Peter Plagens, in *Newsweek*, reviled the "aroma of cultural reparations." Jed Perl, in *The New Criterion*, alleged that the show seemed calculated to get "white male critics into . . . [a] sweat of guilt and remorse and accommodation." Indeed, besides their vitriolic response, these outraged reviewers had something else in common: they were all white men.

To the injury the critics inflicted, add the insult hurled by the outraged museumgoer: "I had been sold a ticket to an art show," one Morton I. Teicher wrote to the editor of *The New York Times*. "This exhibition had nothing to do with art. What redeems the Whitney is that the staff member on duty returned my money without protest."

The response was raw, almost visceral. The arguments have a familiar ring, echoing early objections to modernism and abstraction, determined to preserve the sanctity of art: the work is not beautiful, it's not pleasing, and—the ultimate disqualification—it's not art. This last crossed a line when it came to Whitney Biennials. Gober, by now a veteran of six, says that in other years the critics might question the selection: "People would have their favorites. Why this person? Why not that person? But that's different." In 1993 they were calling into question the artist's legitimacy. "Like, how is this art? Why is this art? What is this doing in a museum?"

Gober tells Sussman during our conversation: "You were very hurt by the reviews is my memory."

"Yeah," she concedes. "I was, you know, surprised."

"And new to New York," Gober adds.

"And new to New York." She'd been nervous about how the *Times* would react. After reading Kimmelman's review, "I had to have two shrink calls before I got out of bed. And then my next port of call was Elizabeth Arden," the spa on Fifth Avenue, where she got a facial. "And then finally I went to work."

Ross had received a call that morning at eight a.m. from Leonard A. Lauder, chairman of the Whitney's board and the museum's longtime benefactor, wanting to know what they were going to do about the review. "And I said, 'It's a terrific exhibition and it will find its place,'" Ross recalls. "But it was hard: Elisabeth felt like she had let me down, though nothing could have been further from the truth."

At the office, she talked to her team. Ross's enthusiasm was, she says, "our buffer with the board." Museums have since become more corporate and more responsive to outside pressures. "I really think in today's environment the people who had done a show like the '93 Biennial would probably be fired," she observes.

If Sussman didn't cry on her colleagues' shoulders, it was because she felt responsible to them, particularly those who had worked with her on the show—and to Golden in particular. "The 1993 Biennial was the first time in my life working on a big exhibition, so for me everything was happening at such an intense level, and Elisabeth is the person who led me through it," Golden says. "I was really wrestling with what this meant with regard to many of the ideas that I cared about and the fact that an art world I very much wanted to be a voice in was rejecting many of the values that were important to me—or that I quite literally represented. Elisabeth was incredibly protective of me, almost as if she hadn't curated the exhibition. She helped me manage that professional moment with care and detachment."

How did she cope? "You know," Sussman says, looking back, "I guess I must have had a certain disdain for what these people were saying that kept me going."

In a career that had strung together one acclaimed exhibition after another, the Biennial was her first brush with what felt like failure, and it happened not in some out-of-the-way venue, but on a big stage with the full attention of the art world. She put it behind her. She'd already identified a few next projects regarding artists whose work she thought deserved to be more widely known, and she dove into them.

## 6

As contemporary art continues to rise in value, museums often find themselves at a disadvantage when it comes to buying new work, priced out of a market crowded with private collectors whose resources exceed the budgets of nonprofit institutions. As a result, they rely increasingly on donations to build their collections. This, too, is part of Sussman's job: to work with a committee of trustees to expand and guide the Whitney's holdings in photography. "Our funds are so limited that, in order to grow this collection, we have to do it very strategically," Sussman says.

The Whitney's board is divided into committees, each concerned with a particular medium: there's a council for painting and sculpture, another for drawing, one for video, and one for photography, chaired by Sondra Gilman, a prominent collector and the museum's longest-serving trustee. "The photography committee is unique in having at the head of it a collector who is deeply invested in the medium," Sussman says. "That's really the ideal situation."

A small, elegant woman of indeterminate age, Gilman lives in an Upper East Side town house with her husband, Celso Gonzalez-Falla; Angus, a Wheaton terrier and self-appointed security guard whose menacing bark rapidly gives way to indiscriminate displays of affection; and a remarkable collection of contemporary art, including, to the right of the living-room fireplace, her 1976 portrait by Andy Warhol.

"I don't want to get too close to artists, because I'm afraid that if I love them, I'll no longer have a dispassionate eye when it comes to their work," she explains. That said, the night of our visit in early December the banister has been festooned with an evergreen garland in preparation for her annual holiday party, which is attended by a large swath of the art world. Over the years a sense of community has coalesced around her deep appreciation for photography.

Gilman majored in art at Syracuse University and began acquiring photographs in the early seventies, when she bought three Eugène Atgets for $250 each. She was young, and everybody told her she was crazy. "Photography isn't an art form," they said. She ignored them and kept going, acting as her own curator rather than relying on some acknowledged expert's advice about what to buy. As time went on and she saw more art, her instincts sharpened.

In 1977 she joined the board of the Whitney. There was no committee for photography acquisitions. She launched a campaign to persuade the museum to collect what was still considered an illegitimate art, to no avail. Meanwhile, with her first husband, Charles Gilman Jr., she assembled on behalf of Gilman Paper Company, the family business, a photography collection recognized today as one of the finest in the world.

Finally, in 1991, with David Ross as director and Leonard Lauder as head of the board, the Whitney came around: "They told me, 'Okay, Sondra, your time has come. Go for it.'" She resigned from the painting and sculpture committee and transferred her energies to building the museum's photography collection, with Sussman as her collaborator. Both felt the weight of their responsibility.

"We should have a history of American photography within the Whitney," Sussman says, "because we have a history of American art. We should have deep Robert Frank, deep Gary Winogrand, deep Diane Arbus. And then, going back, we should have deep Walker Evans and Edward

Weston, because all those have parallels in our painting and sculpture.

"One thing we came to realize at a certain point in the nineties," she continues, "was that there was a group of undervalued photographers who have come to be recognized as the New York School, and that if we as the Whitney Museum of American Art sitting right here in New York didn't have a good representation of their work, then something was wrong. So we went after that very seriously." There was still a lot of good work available and affordable.

The early masters, however, were another story. By then, if a vintage print by Edward Weston or Walker Evans came on the market, it was $250,000—far beyond what the museum could afford. "We just couldn't touch great vintage photography before 1950," Sussman says. Gilman's own collection, however, was strong in that early period. Together, she and Sussman chose from it seventy-five vintage images, nineteen of them by Evans. All are now eventually destined for the Whitney.

Gilman calls herself a "purist" in that she only collects photographs printed within five years of the negative, in an effort to honor the photographer's original intent. When it came to early color photography, however, the policy proved untenable. "We ran into a problem with the work of Stephen Shore," Sussman says. A New York photographer who shot in color in the seventies, Shore used film that didn't last: the colors bleached and the images faded, not unlike most people's family snapshots of the period. So Shore agreed to reprint a selection of his work. "I think that's probably the only way we're going to get him into the collection," Sussman says. Having established the policy, she and Gilman understood that the time had come to make an exception to it.

Today the committee holds three purchasing meetings a year, for which Gilman and Sussman prepare in advance to make their case for work they want to acquire. When Gilman is buying for herself, she puts her own enthusiasm first. "It's like I've fallen in love," she explains. Her instinct at this point is the product of long years of looking and buying. However, when she's thinking about what to acquire for the Whitney, the selection process is different. "It's what they need, what they don't have," she says. The choices she and Sussman make on behalf of the museum, she says, "will be judged by posterity."

Each of the thirty-five members of the photography committee makes an annual $10,000 contribution; the total is their budget for the year. While this may sound like a lot of money, it doesn't go far. In fact, it could easily be spent on a single photograph. The debate over what to buy is, in Sussman's words, "a killer." But from the outset she and Gilman agreed that they didn't want a committee that would serve as a mere rubber stamp, so they recognize that the discussion, no matter how difficult, is crucial to its function.

Sometimes Sussman's recommendations fail to get the necessary votes. "But then," she says, "I always think that the committee is like the public in that if you can't convince this group of educated people that something's important for the Whitney, then how do you convince everyone else?"

Still, Gilman says, it's not uncommon for Sussman to present photographs already familiar to members of the committee and for her insights to change their point of view. Asked to characterize Sussman's manner in making these pitches, Gilman says she's never confrontational. "And there's no arrogance. You would think that with her knowledge and her history, she would come and announce, 'Okay, this is it.' But she doesn't do that."

"Because I don't feel that way, that's why," Sussman responds. "I'm uncertain all the time about these choices. I mean, I work with wonderful people and everybody has a strong point of view and there's a limited pot and it's a dynamic situation. So I'm never sure that what I think we should do is right." Still, no one has done more to determine the Whitney's permanent collection in photography, with choices that will shape future generations' understanding of the form and its place in our time.

## 7

Most curators choose their own subjects on the basis of ideas or artists that they're drawn to. In rare cases, the relationship becomes so close and the curator so invested that a show takes on the quality of a crusade. This phenomenon has occurred in Sussman's career more often than not.

At one point in the early 1990s she decided that, going forward, she would curate only exhibitions by women artists. Immersed in preparations for two massive retrospectives that still stand as monuments to the women they featured, she was determined to remedy the fact that their work was underappreciated and insufficiently understood. Both had died prematurely: Eva Hesse, at thirty-four, in 1970; and Diane Arbus, at forty-eight, in 1971.

Like many others in the New York art world, Sussman made a pilgrimage to New Haven in 1992 to see an exhibition of works by Hesse organized by Helen Achbar Cooper, curator of American paintings and sculpture at the Yale University Art Gallery. Hesse was already legendary, and the outline of her tragic life was widely known: the flight from Nazi Germany with her sister as the daughters of German Jews; their reunion with their parents; her parents' divorce and her mother's subsequent suicide; and her own career cut short, after only a decade, by a malignant brain tumor. She was highly regarded as an artist, one of the only women of the post-minimalist generation to sit at the table with the guys.

"I had known her work," Sussman says, "but when I read the catalog and saw the show, I was completely amazed." Back at the Whitney, she checked to see how much of Hesse's work was in the museum's collection. Then she discovered that Hesse had never had a New York City show. "I thought it was time."

Sussman was looking for some aspect of Hesse's story that hadn't been told. A 1972 biography by Lucy Lippard, a feminist art historian and friend of Hesse's, focused on the circle of 1960s downtown artists she had been a part of and the difficulty of making her way as a woman in the art world. But, Sussman noted, "one thing that struck me: no one had really recognized what Hesse had been through as this European child, the impact of the Holocaust and what it did to her family. So it was very important to me to take that on." There were German Jews who, like Hesse's family, had come from Hamburg during the exodus and settled in Washington Heights, a neighborhood in northern Manhattan, in the late 1930s. "So there were people still around who could describe what Hesse's family had experienced," Sussman says.

And then came the real find: records kept by Hesse's father, a lawyer prevented by the Nazis from practicing. "He was one of these meticulous German scrapbook keepers," Sussman continues. "He wasn't alone. There were many people like him who made *Tagebuch*s—literally, day books or journals."

Helen Charash, Hesse's sister, calls them "such an important look into our background and our childhood. My father started one for each of us when we were born and continued them until I was twelve. There were three of Eva's and five or six of mine." Entries include day-to-day information, news clippings, and pictures—Mr. Hesse was an amateur photographer—intended as personal history for his daughters, so that they would have a record of the times in which their early lives had unfolded. Helen was five and a half and Eva just short of three years old when they left, without their parents, on the Kindertransport, as part of a Nazi initiative after Kristallnacht to ship Jewish children out of Germany. Helen had kept the *Tagebuch*s, and no one had ever looked at them. "I opened up to Elisabeth everything I had," she says.

With a love of research and a capacity for empathy that would serve any biographer well, Sussman delved into Hesse's experience. "It's the most plaintive story," she says. It was also one in a series of instances when a subject has essentially hijacked Sussman's brain and taken over her life. Thelma Golden says that, "given the depth with which she engages certain artists' work, she becomes not just an expert in the work but in the world around the work as well."

Hesse married a sculptor, who was not Jewish. Together they went to Germany in 1966 on a fellowship he'd been granted, and she visited Hamburg and the other towns that her family had fled. "Her first breakthrough work was there," according to Sussman.

Hesse was by all accounts a quietly charismatic figure. "Whoever gets seriously involved with her work gets pulled in," Charash says, "not only on a professional level but on an emotional and human level, too. No one did work as long and complete as Elisabeth. It wasn't just research. Her heart and soul were in it, too."

"In her tenacious, unrelenting, implacable way, Elisabeth was tracking down every possible lead that would help her to illuminate Eva and her work," says Tony Ganz, the Los Angeles collector, whose parents had known Hesse and acquired a number of her drawings and sculptures.

In another round of the ongoing game of musical chairs that characterizes the art world at its highest echelons, David Ross was fired from the Whitney in 1998 and replaced by Maxwell Anderson, who'd been directing Toronto's Art Gallery of Ontario. The Whitney curators took turns filling Anderson in on projects already in the works. When Sussman's turn came, she told him about Hesse and Arbus. Each show, in its own way, would be a coup for the museum: Hesse because she'd never had a museum show in New York and because her sculptures in particular, in various stages of decay due to their materials, so rarely traveled; Arbus because there'd been no exhibition since the Museum of Modern Art's, two years after her death and some twenty-five years prior. In both cases Sussman had the wholehearted cooperation of the artists' estates—of Helen Charash, Eva's sister, and Doon Arbus, Diane's daughter—which was by no means automatic, given their concerns about how the work would be displayed and the way the artist would be represented. Anderson politely informed Sussman that he wasn't interested, and Hesse and Arbus were struck from the Whitney's calendar of upcoming exhibitions.

When word got out, people in museum and gallery circles were aghast. Both in-depth, long-term projects—tributes to two New York artists—were "shows that needed to happen," according to one former curator at a rival institution, "and they needed to happen in New York." Sussman was undeterred. Anderson's verdict in essence obliged her to choose between her work and her job. She chose her work and left the Whitney, trading in the security of a museum position and a salary for the vagaries of freelancing. She took the Hesse and Arbus shows to San Francisco's Museum of Modern Art, where David Ross had landed as the new director.

Planning for the Hesse exhibition proved to be even more complex than usual, due to the sculptures' fragility and the ephemeral nature of the materials she used, like rope and fiberglass. In particular, Hesse loved the unique properties of latex, which she discovered and began to explore in 1967—its capacity to conform to a shape but remain flexible, to register the imprint of any surface it touched. The color could be neutral or manipulated with the addition of pigment; variations in thickness could range from translucent to opaque, depending on how many layers were applied.

These materials' eventual obsolescence proved to be as much a practical issue as a philosophical one. "The question is: Did Hesse know that latex sculpture would deteriorate?" Sussman writes. "Would she have accepted the process of deterioration, and would she allow it to be visible over time? Might she enjoy the analogies that this process of decay has to the fate of things in the world and consciously incorporate them into the content of her work? A central problem raised by works not necessarily designed for longevity is that at some point their status as an artwork may come to an end . . . Hesse's latex works were *something*; at what point would they become *nothing*, and was this a status she wanted for them?"

In February 2002 the show opened. Sussman succeeded in bringing together an unprecedented amount of Hesse's work—more than had ever been seen in one place. It was Sussman's idea to juxtapose her paintings, sculptures, and works on paper, since Hesse often developed the same idea in parallel forms. Because many of the pieces had seldom traveled due to their delicate condition, people knew them only from photographs, if at all. For those already familiar with Hesse and her work, the impact of seeing so much of it in person, coupled with Sussman's findings on her life, forced a reconsideration of what they thought they already knew. For those encountering Hesse's work for the first time, the show was not only an introduction to the artist, but a demonstration of her heroic attempts to transcend the art of her own time. "I would like the work to be non-work," she wrote. "This means that it would find its way beyond my preconceptions . . . It is my main concern to go beyond what I know and what I can know . . ."

There was a vaguely tenuous quality to Hesse's sculpture, made from these strange materials that did not aspire to permanence, the kind of immortality conferred by metal and stone. As with so many of the shows that Sussman conceives and orchestrates, spectators came away with a sense of having encountered something full of meaning but unsure what to make of it. Without nailing down ideas that want to soar, Sussman's catalog essay helpfully articulates the conundrum at the heart of the work. "Hesse became consumed by a desire to move beyond what was considered sculpture, or, in the parlance of the 1960s, 'objects,'" Sussman writes. "She struggled to realize creations of another status, material things in the world that she termed 'non-art' . . . The artwork is amorphous and strangely beautiful as it hovers between something and nothing."

ike many curators, Sussman has come to be identified with the artists she has presented. Her commitment to them continues long after the exhibitions have ended and the catalogs have been published. She revisits their work, and her understanding of it keeps on evolving. New insights add more layers of appreciation.

In 2003, just six months after her Hesse exhibition closed, Sussman's show on Diane Arbus opened in the same galleries at the San Francisco Museum of Modern Art. It was the first thorough reexamination of Arbus's work since the landmark retrospective at New York's Museum of Modern Art in 1972, the year after her death. In the interim, all manner of speculation about Arbus, her motives, and her regard (or supposed lack of it) for the people she photographed had poisoned the air around the work. The quasi-anthropological curiosity Arbus brought to her fellow humans and the way they sorted themselves into subcultures, with a neutral gaze that passed no judgment, was condemned as unsparing, lacking compassion and tact, exposing people who might otherwise have remained invisible.

Among her most outspoken detractors was Susan Sontag, whose 1973 essay, "Freak Show," published in the *New York Review of Books*, turned the tide. Sontag presented her chief objection to Arbus's pictures on moral grounds, claiming that they violated the people they portrayed. "Armed with a camera," Sontag contended, Arbus "could insinuate anguish, kinkiness, mental illness with any subject," even babies, and this was unethical because the people had somehow consented to be photographed without realizing how ugly or grotesque they looked. (This assumes that subjects are entitled to a becoming likeness, a notion worth debating.) Sontag attributed this act of aggression to the fact that Arbus was a fashion photographer, obliged to produce pretty images of beautiful women—as if "fashion photographer" were a type, despite the fact that all sorts of photographers, many of them "serious" or "art" photographers, worked in fashion at the time because the assignments were well paid. And then there's Arbus's suicide, triggering what Sontag deplored as "a kind of apotheosis," as if the overriding significance of her untimely death were not the fact that she lost her battle with a persistent sense of hopelessness but that ending her life proved to be an effective career strategy.

In response and in defense of her mother, Doon Arbus closed the door on any situations she couldn't entirely control. Among people in the art world, the Arbus estate became notorious for saying no. Arbus's reputation went into eclipse as a result of Doon's determination to protect the work from the received opinions and foregone conclusions that had enveloped it.

"The photographs needed me," she later wrote. "Well, they needed someone. Someone to keep track of them, to safeguard them—however unsuccessfully—from an onslaught of theory and interpretation, as if translating images into words were the only way to make them visible."

Sussman's show marked a departure from this embargo. Over a research phase that lasted nine years, she earned Doon's trust as they combed through Arbus's agendas, letters, notebooks, snapshots, and other memorabilia. The resulting book and exhibition, which integrated the photographs and an annotated chronology that functioned as a de facto autobiography, signaled not "a change of heart," Doon wrote in the catalog's afterword, "but one of strategy, and a willingness to embrace the paradox: that this surfeit of information and opinion would finally render the scrim of words invisible so that anyone encountering the photographs could meet them in the eloquence of their silence."

As an intimate record of Arbus's thoughts and preoccupations, the entries provided viewers with the means to situate her photographs in the context of her life. A postcard to a friend in 1960: "I think it does, a little, hurt to be photographed." In a notebook a year later: "Anxiety is fear looking for a cause." From an award presented by the American Society of Magazine Photographers in 1970: "for her revelation of truth in the 'found' individual, who might not be noticed, otherwise, by the less observant." Although the show's title, *Revelations*, ran the risk of hyperbole, in the end it was justified by the evidence.

By introducing information about Arbus's life, the chronology might easily have capsized. But the presentation made no attempt to interpret events or coax emotion from the viewer. Even the bold decision to end with the autopsy, which is not for the squeamish, was in keeping with the dispassionate presentation. "That was ultimately, you know, a fact," Sussman says—a fact whose clinical understatement triggers sorrow on the part of the reader.

Robert Gober, who has himself curated small exhibitions

over the years, notes that there are movements in curating, just as there are movements in art. "There are movements toward just showing the things themselves, without much explanation," he says, on the grounds that the work should speak for itself. "And then there's a different school of thought: that art illustrates biography, or biography illustrates art. That somehow, through biography, you get the answers to the art. But you can go way wrong with that."

In my conversation with him and Sussman, we discussed the ideal life-to-art ratio for the purpose of illuminating the work. "Well, I think one thing I've learned from working with you, Bob," Sussman tells him, "is that ultimately it's all mystery. When you come to the realization that no biography, no wall text, no nothing, is going to tell you what you want to know exactly, that's when the magic begins."

Two weeks after the *Untitled* show opened, Sussman and I return to David Zwirner's gallery to get a second look. A handful of people are making their way around the three rooms, talking in hushed tones as if they were in a church, moving as people in galleries do, facing the walls and stepping sideways. Staring at art alongside Sussman, you realize that she sees more of what she's looking at than most people do. And that, after most people would have moved on to the next image, she's still there, still looking, long past the point where you think you've taken everything in.

We begin our tour of the first room in front of a photo of a woman wearing a printed cotton housedress and ankle socks, in a field bordered in the background by trees. She is standing in the nearest of three long shadows—shallow diagonals that enter the picture plane from the right. A few dried leaves scattered on the grass indicate that it's fall.

"For some reason," Sussman says, "I always focus on peripheral things first, so I look at the time of day, the shadows, the kind of feelings Arbus gets out of the land-scape through these grays and blacks and these big empty spaces. And then: What would she have thought looking at this woman? That's one thing. What do I think looking at her? That's another. Undeniably, this is a female, at an age beyond puberty. The bodies and the faces here give you different information, because the faces and the heads make it clear that these people are different from us. But then their bodies speak their own language, too. This woman's body is incongruous with her face, I think, caught in some stage between infant and adult." Individually and collectively, Sussman says, the *Untitled* images call into question notions we take for granted: "What is age? What's the body? What's the mind? What's sexuality?"

The clothes the people in the pictures wear are clearly castoffs and hand-me-downs, in styles some twenty years behind the time of the photos. "They look uncannily like the way people dress now if they've gone to a lot of thrift shops," Sussman says. "Somebody commented to me at the opening that because there's this nostalgia for vintage in fashion, some of these people, perversely, look stylish now in a way they didn't then."

We come to Arbus's view of an interior—a room with a linoleum floor and a low ceiling containing a picnic table, a wagon, two chairs, and three figures: one, wearing a dress and what looks like lipstick, her hair in a bowl cut, her eyes rolled back into her head; one lying on the floor with an inverted chair perched on her knees; the third, seated in the background, busy with some motion, oblivious to the camera. Each seems isolated in his or her own world; there is no interaction with or even awareness of the others. Nor do they engage with the photographer.

"This is a very strange, disturbing picture," Sussman says. "When Arbus first got this project in mind, this was the first asylum that she was let into. So she did these interiors."

Sussman then points out something I hadn't noticed—that everything is slightly off-kilter; nothing is level or plumb. Arbus's camera is tilted a few degrees, just enough to skew the axis where the two walls meet in the corner, to tilt the horizontals where the wall meets the ceiling and the floor. The effect is subliminally disorienting, a signal that this is a world in which the law of gravity has been quietly subverted.

Arbus didn't return to that first facility once she was granted access to a home for mentally retarded adults in Vineland, New Jersey, where most of these pictures were taken, because, according to Sussman, she was so thrilled with the grounds there and the light. There's a pastoral quality to the landscape, which serves as a tenebrous backdrop. Holidays were big occasions. Arbus photographed at picnics, dances, Halloween. The residents wear masks or wizards' hats or bunny ears, rendering the peculiar even more bizarre. Four masked figures sporting white smocks that look as if they've been fashioned from organdy curtains each hold a wand with a cut-paper star at the end; there are cutout stars on their paper crowns and on their shoes. Another group makes its way across the foreground of a twilit field, the bright white of their pajamas and nightgowns standing out in stark relief against the dark tree line and silver clouds. Sussman studies the image more closely for clues to how Arbus achieved the contrasts—possibly with a flash or a strobe, which she used even in daylight. Throughout this series, Sussman says, she was experimenting with a variety of techniques: "The magic of these prints is what she got in the tonalities. The grayscale on this is just so beautiful."

In an essay accompanying these photos, collected in a book in 1995, Doon Arbus writes about the breakthrough they represent in her mother's evolution as a photographer: "Where her best-known work challenges us to look, or seduces us into looking, these photographs simply disclose themselves, as if content to be discovered. Her presence, once the invisible center of her pictures, the thing you couldn't see and couldn't ignore, is now subsumed within the image and goes all but unnoticed. The collaborator has become a witness."

Sussman and I move on to a picture of two women sitting on the grass on a blanket, one with her arm slung over the other's shoulder, both looking straight into the camera. "This forthrightness in being photographed, that's pretty amazing," Sussman remarks. Indeed, the images are striking for the subjects' lack of inhibition. In her portraits of celebrities, Arbus shows them at their most guarded, composing their faces and presenting them to the camera. Here, the force field between the photographer and her subjects is filled with trust and what feels like tenderness.

Arbus herself considered these pictures a breakthrough. In a letter to her ex-husband Allan she wrote: "FINALLY what I've been searching for."

Arbus took 170 images in all for this project before it was cut short by her death; she made finished prints of only 25. Of the additional 41 that Doon selected, few are new to Sussman, who looked at everything in preparation for the show in San Francisco. Various groups of photos from the *Untitled* series have been exhibited previously, but never this many.

While Sussman has been in conversations with collectors about buying the works for the Whitney, the sheer quantity becomes a consideration in thinking about how to show the images in a museum setting. Their impact is cumulative—profound, disturbing, difficult to pinpoint. "What the Whitney would do with this number of pictures is very hard to know," Sussman says. "We're so used to looking at one at a time. You do have to have a mass of them, I think, in order to grasp what's going on in them—the emotions, the intent.

"Why was Arbus photographing these people? Was she not as upset by them as she could have been?" Sussman knows from her research that at the time Arbus was reading R. D. Laing, a psychiatrist who was questioning not only the nature of mental illness but also its diagnosis. "So that's where her mind would go."

On rare occasions and under the very best circumstances, the relationship between artist and curator occupies a unique place in both their lives—more intimate in some respects than friendship or love, with elements of both. The curator earns the artist's trust; the artist admits the curator to that place where the impulse to create resides. A depth of understanding develops, and a complicity. The artist lives inside the work and through it; the curator becomes a wit-ness—in real time or in retrospect—to the struggle to make it, the compression of ideas and emotions as they're trans-formed into art. The curator nurtures the work, situating it in the context of the cultural moment and helping it find its audience, tending it with meticulous care. Even when the artist is deceased, this dynamic—this profound capacity to entertain the artist's intent while seeing the outcome on its own terms—can still occur, as it did in Sussman's relation-ship to Arbus.

"From the experience I've had with Arbus's work now over all these years," she says, "I can see that there's a first reading, where she tells you everything you want to know about people who were sort of odd in the sixties society she lived in. She would go find them and make us look at them. And then I've been lucky enough to have a second stage of interest in Arbus. I realize she's going after something ineffable, and that's in these 'Untitled' photographs. In the atmosphere we're living in and perhaps forever, these photo-graphs are going to have their detractors, but I'm willing to deal with the ambiguities. I say this based on what all curators have to go on: an intuition that something is truly great."

## 9

The career of a curator who works within a museum is often largely dictated by the institution's priorities: showcasing the permanent collection, minding budgets, building an audience. These may prompt certain ideas for exhibitions and preclude others. It might appear that independent curators have more freedom and are able to move from one project and one venue to the next, but, as in other fields, freelancing comes with its own frustrations. Like many curators, Sussman has done both. Having learned the protocol and craft at the Institute of Contemporary Art and the Whitney, she was prompted by circumstance to go out on her own, mounting the Hesse and Arbus shows in San Francisco at Ross's behest. In 2003, with those mammoth projects behind her, she suddenly found herself at a loss, with nothing lined up to follow.

She spent three months as a visiting scholar at the Getty Research Institute in Los Angeles with the idea that she would turn her work on Eva Hesse into a new biography. (When nine years later Marcie Begleiter, a filmmaker, approached her as a potential source for her documentary about Hesse, Sussman magnanimously handed over her research.) She interviewed with a foundation in St. Louis and a museum in Philadelphia. She had a conversation with Gober and Matthew Marks, his gallerist, who had admired the Arbus chronology and were planning to do something along similar lines that would weave together interviews, family history, political events, the onset of the AIDS epidemic, and Gober's activism with his work. "And I would've done that in a flash," she says. But at some point in their conversations Gober wondered aloud whether she shouldn't go back to work at the Whitney, an idea Sussman dismissed at the time.

Shortly thereafter, however, she got a call from Adam Weinberg, her former colleague, who back in the nineties served as head of the Whitney's permanent collection. After sitting out the Anderson years as director of the Addison Gallery of American Art at Phillips Academy, he'd been brought back to the museum in 2003 as its director, and now he was looking to bring her back as well. "And I was just stopped in my tracks," she says. She promised him a decision within twenty-four hours, although now, she says, she wonders why it took her even that long to think about it.

Among veterans of the Whitney's tumultuous years, Weinberg has earned a reputation as a peacemaker, reconciling factions on the board and among the staff, leading the museum, with the move to its new home in Manhattan's Meatpacking District, into a lively new era. As he talks about Sussman, it becomes clear that he brought her back not only because he admires what she's accomplished but also because, corporate mission statements aside, her working notion of the role a museum plays in society is a model for what he wants the Whitney to be.

Sussman accepted Weinberg's offer and returned. On her first day back, she found on her desk a present from Thelma Golden: a plexiglass frame holding one of Daniel Martinez's badges from their '93 Biennial. This one had a single word: "IMAGINE."

"You're in the midst of a contradiction," Weinberg says. "The institution is the establishment, and at the same time you're representing minority points of view. I don't mean that in any ethnic or racial sense. I mean points of view that people don't think are necessarily worth considering. And it takes a curator like Elisabeth to understand these positions and open the public's eyes to them."

Weinberg cites as examples two of the artists she has championed—Gordon Matta-Clark and Paul Thek—whose work was widely considered marginal; their posthumous retrospectives, which Sussman mounted at the Whitney in 2007 and 2010, respectively, have since consolidated their places in history. "They made some beautiful objects, but their work goes far beyond beauty and far beyond the objects. It's a marriage of the objects and ideas in a profound way that fundamentally shifts things." Sussman, Weinberg says, has "a very clear vision of what an artist *does*. It's not a case of the institution transforming the artist. It's the artist trying to transform the institution. That is a very difficult process—often exciting and at other times painful—but that is the dilemma of being in a contemporary art museum in a capitalist society."

In 2015 the Whitney's staff took up residency in the new building designed by Renzo Piano. Sussman now occupies a small office in a corner of the seventh floor. A glass wall separates her and other curators from the maze of cubicles where the curatorial assistants sit. She has no window, but if you stick your head out her office door and look to the right, you can see the West Side Highway and the new public park under construction on Pier 55. The décor is modernist non-profit—all white with wood accents and gray wall-to-wall carpet. The footprint is minimal, even cramped, with the only sense of space overhead: Sussman's office, like others, is higher than it is wide. The routine correlation between success and square footage doesn't apply here. Copies of Sussman's own catalogs appear among the books arranged on shelves that run the length of two adjacent walls, most of them so high as to be out of reach without a ladder; more books are stacked on her desk and arranged in piles on a table. An enormous poster from Mike Kelley's 2006 show at the Louvre dominates one wall. Pinned to the felt-covered corkboard above her desk is a postcard that reads: "THE POINT IS NOT TO PUT POETRY AT THE DISPOSAL OF THE REVOLUTION BUT TO PUT THE REVOLUTION AT THE DISPOSAL OF POETRY."

From a spectator's point of view, all museums might look alike, or at least similar. In fact, the administrative structure can have a huge bearing on individual careers, especially in their early stages. As chief curator, Rothkopf made the decision to promote more people rather than keep them at the secretarial level—to hand them a ladder they could begin to climb. Over four years, he has elevated some ten assistants into curatorial positions. He has also instituted salary increases and paid internships. "Traditionally, these jobs have gone to trust-fund kids," Sussman acknowledges. Only those who could afford to work without pay applied, which made for a workforce that was overwhelmingly white and privileged. A living wage could help diversify the pipeline, eventually transforming not only the composition of the workforce but also the points of view represented, the expertise on hand, and ultimately the art that gets shown.

Since then, the number of applicants for the Whitney's internships—which span the entire museum, including not only the curatorial department but also finance, fundraising, and facilities—has "gone through the roof," Scott Rothkopf says, and the backgrounds they come from are far more diverse. Thelma Golden, in her current capacity as director of the Studio Museum in Harlem, visits schools in the neighborhood, where there's a slogan on the wall: "You have to see it to be it." Now they see her.

Rothkopf sidesteps any suggestion that he has been responsible for making the museum better able to reflect the world outside its walls. "This wasn't something I just came up with," he says. "There were ideas that you should have curators of color going back to the 1960s. For me, it was more a feeling that we were responsible to these ideals, that we had to try and act by them, and maybe we hadn't been acting by them to the best of our abilities."

Rothkopf acknowledges that the landscape has shifted considerably. "The kinds of people who are interested in art are changing, and what they're expecting from museums is changing in ways that I think are positive but sometimes also difficult to fulfill," he says. Whereas a certain kind of intellectual glamour might once have served as the impetus for entering the art world for a career, "now people are more thinking about questions to do with social justice—about how art can be a space for thinking differently about the world, for asking really hard critical questions. And they're often hoping that museums can be a model of this society that they might like better than the one in which they exist."

n 2010, Adam Weinberg asked Sussman to curate another Biennial—this one for 2012. Portfolios of young curators qualified to be her collaborators were gathered and sent her way. But Sussman had another idea. She called Jay Sanders, who was directing Greene Naftali, a gallery in Chelsea, and working with film, video, and experimental musicians. They had met on two occasions: when she wanted to learn more about one of the gallery's artists and Sanders gave her some materials, then again when he walked her through the gallery's booth at an art fair—all in a day's work if you're an art dealer. But, Sanders says, for him the connection was more meaningful. "She's someone who was, in her own way, a bit mythic to me as a curator. She's not the most public person. And she doesn't perform herself as a persona in the art world. She works quietly and has close confidants." From time to time he would text her the name of a book he'd just read that dovetailed with one of their earlier conversations.

Then, out of the blue, Sussman called to ask Sanders if he would be able to step away from his job for a while if something came up. They met for coffee in the East Village. "And without a beat, she said, 'Would you create a Whitney Biennial with me?'" Sanders recalls. "I was taken aback." The prospect of working for a museum had never occurred to him. It was rare at the time, he says, for someone to "jump the track" from the more commercial, gallery side of the art world to the nonprofit realm of museums. "And I wasn't a trained art historian," he added.

"You're a bit of an unlikely choice," Sussman admitted. Sanders says he grappled with the decision to take a sabbatical from the roster of artists he'd built. But in the end he concluded that "it's one of those things that you can't say no to. I was really honored, because I held her in such high esteem. And I trusted her. If she thought I could do it, I thought, 'Well, I guess I have to take that in.'"

As a way to get acquainted, they decided that instead of simply trading lists of favorites artists, they would invite each other into their respective intellectual worlds. For starters, Sanders arranged a visit to his friend John Zorn, the musician, who "knows a lot about progressive culture in New York and the underground." She proposed that they call on her friend Greil Marcus, the rock critic who puts music in the larger context of social and political developments. "Not that these people would be in the show," Sanders says. "But we went through this process for the first month or two of meeting the people with whom we check in on a personal level, just getting to know each other through our intimates."

Their exhibition, though by no means the head-on confrontation that so many critics took the 1993 Biennial to be, was nonetheless radical in its own way: they removed the walls on the museum's top floor and made it a dedicated space for performance and what Sanders calls "time-based work"; they collaborated with artists who themselves curated small shows within the larger exhibition; they tapped into the energy of Occupy Wall Street and young artists' renewed sense of activism. The Biennial became a premise for meeting with the artists they admired, like Werner Herzog, who in the end contributed an installation interleaving clips from his films with projections of phantasmagorical landscapes by Hercules Segers, a seventeenth-century Dutch artist.

"Jay and I were both interested in performance and film and making them more central to the art discussion,"

Sussman says. "We shared an interest in particular artists," Kelley and Gober among them. "We balanced each other, led each other in funny directions, gave each other the courage to be very ambitious. We also shared a disinterest in the big bad art world," she says dryly.

She and Sanders had no expectations for how the show would be received. "We felt it was going to be a sort of anti-spectacular, non-blockbuster, somewhat hermetic kind of show," he says. "We figured if we like it, if it's satisfying the two of us, who are not hard on each other but hard on ourselves and skeptical of this whole form—if we're building a show that we would want to see, then that's the best we can do."

This time around, the critics loved it. Noting the long tradition of dismissive reviews for Biennials past, Peter Schjeldahl wrote in *The New Yorker*: "Here's an untried epithet: 'enchanting.'" References to 1993 were inevitable, given Sussman's involvement. But a funny thing had happened over the intervening two decades: the culture had caught up with the show that had gone down in infamy.

Themes of otherness, identity, and the body, which she had located just beneath the surface in 1993, had emerged as pivotal issues in the national conversation. Sussman's first

Biennial began to look not misguided, as the critics had claimed at the time, but prescient. Race, gender, sexuality, and the discrimination that surrounded them were now out in the open, exposed. A number of artists on the roster—including Janine Antoni, Matthew Barney, Sadie Benning, Peter Cain, Renée Green, Byron Kim, Daniel Martinez, Mark Rappaport, Gary Simmons, Sue Williams, Charles Ray, Guillermo Gómez-Peña, and Coco Fusco—who were brought to the attention of a major museum audience in the '93 show had since risen to prominence. Far from being forgotten or remembered as a failure, the '93 Biennial had over time become a touchstone.

In 2013 the New Museum (under the direction of Lisa Phillips, a member of Sussman's 1993 curatorial team) mounted *NYC 1993: Experimental Jet Set, Trash and No Star.* (The subtitle is borrowed from an album by Sonic Youth.) As a time capsule of sorts, bringing together work exhibited in New York during that pivotal year, the show occasioned reflection and soul-searching. In the rearview mirror, the '93 Biennial took on a different aspect: the scandal receded, and the show was recast as a success.

"I resisted the truth that it embodied a necessary force of history, squaring the little art world with big values of democracy," wrote Peter Schjeldahl, acknowledging that he had changed his mind. "But truth will tell, and I came around. Art survived just fine. The event was good for society, and gradually, by the way, for me."

Bridget R. Cooks, author of *Exhibiting Blackness: African Americans and the American Art Museum*, called out "identity politics," the categorical grounds on which the show was initially condemned, as the term "used to degrade work that critics did not want to spend time understanding because it dealt with histories that they believed did not belong."

"Establishment art history circa 1993 was a broken model," Jerry Saltz wrote in *New York Magazine*, "built on white men and Western civilization and on ossified ideas about 'greatness' and 'genius.'" For Saltz, that Biennial was "the moment in which today's art world was born." Identity and the body— the '93 Biennial's central themes—emerged as "central themes of the decade," Saltz said. "Some embraced that new reality in order to move forward; others reacted against it. The Biennial was on the side of the future, and still is."

SUSSMAN'S LONE INSTANCE OF abject failure was now hailed as a game changer. "I think Biennials in general are kind of destined to fail," David Joselit says, "but 1993 is now a major historical point of reference. To do something that defines the era, it's not enough that it's a good show; it has to be synchronized with the questions people are thinking about. In '93, Elisabeth found the issues." Her Biennial had come out on the right side of history.

Even for Thelma Golden two decades after the fact, the most traumatic experience of her early career was at least partially redeemed by what had gone on since. "We stirred up a lot of issues that were and continue to be central issues in American life. That experience was extremely painful, because no one likes to be at the center of a big critical media storm. But on the other hand, it showed me, first, that the museum could stand behind it and tackle such a controversy and, following the show, that the museum could actually in many ways change its program and its collection to reflect what had gone on in that Biennial."

Less obvious, perhaps, but no less important, Sussman's 1993 show broke new ground in terms of procedure. The artists did what they wanted to do. Reviews of prior Biennials routinely kept score—six artists from this gallery, five from that one—as a way of ranking the most powerful dealers. Sussman ended that practice.

One might think that Sussman's decision to remain a lifelong curator would limit the scope of her influence, but even from her position within the ranks, she exerts a certain idea about what the museum should be and how it should function. "She has great respect for what an institution is supposed to do," Sanders says. "She actually values what a museum is and its social function and its relationship to other aspects of the art world. It's an institutional morality, all these things that sound like Whitney rhetoric: a certain risk taking, a certain trust in visionary and slightly eccentric form. She advocates for important artistic positions that are undervalued and overlooked and feel essential."

## 11

Like many curators, Sussman juggles several projects at a time, in various stages of development. The process of mounting an exhibition, from inception to opening, can take a few months to several years, encompassing extensive research, lengthy negotiations, complex loan arrangements, plans for a tour, placement of the work in the galleries, production of a catalog and writing an essay for it, and drafting wall text. The lead curator must oversee it all. Exhibitions can be enormous logistical feats, and the curator's job requires efficient project management. In addition to the intellectual and creative challenges of conceiving a show, there is a sizable amount of administrative work and the day-to-day minutiae of inching all the pieces forward.

As of December 2018, Sussman was roughly ten months away from the debut of her next exhibition, a retrospective of the career of Rachel Harrison, an American artist highly regarded within the art world and little known beyond it.

Her work references art history, pop culture, consumerism, and celebrity. Her sculptures, which in many cases start as Styrofoam covered in cement, are then painted, often in vivid colors. Many incorporate unusual materials and objects—canned peas, a water cooler, a video monitor—and some sly note of humor, in an attempt to create what Harrison calls "shapes that can't be described." Not that that stops anyone from trying. The conversation surrounding her work inverts terms like "junk" and "clumsy-looking" as high praise; some fervent admirers claim a 180-degree conversation experience, from not just skepticism but initial revulsion.

The choice of Harrison is in keeping with Sussman's penchant for artists whose work is not easily accessible by virtue of its beauty or its obvious ideas. "She's interested in artists who are inventing their form in eccentric ways," Sanders says. "It's a certain kind of intellectual bricolage that comes out of subcultural interests and complex practices. She's attracted to artists who are a little irascible about the world we all live in. Hard artists. Rachel is a hard artist."

ON A FRIDAY MORNING, Sussman joins members of her team for the Harrison show to review the catalog layout with Joseph Logan, the book's designer. In a conference room behind a glass wall, they gather in plain sight of the visitors milling around the adjacent gallery—as if the workings of the museum had been put on display like the gears of a clock in a glass case. At the far end of the table, Logan sits in front of a large screen on the wall on which images from two laptops are projected. David Joselit, who will be giving a lecture on Harrison, and Sussman occupy one side of the table, opposite Beth Turk, the Whitney's editor, and Gustavo Gordillo, an emissary from Harrison's studio; Kelly Long, Sussman's assistant, sits at the near end, taking notes. While the temperature of the conversation is respectful and cordial, Gordillo firmly asserts Harrison's positions.

Logan clicks through the layouts: a grid of images from Harrison's *31 Sunsets*; two photos of a hand pressed against the glass inside the window of a house in Perth Amboy, where the Virgin Mary was rumored to have appeared; a picture of a bright pink pole supporting a giant pink arrow pointing diagonally down to a Henry Moore bronze in a plaza behind the city hall in Dallas. Another sculpture, quite tall, is depicted sideways, across two pages.

Sussman stops when they come to a photo of a sculpture called *Blind Bunnies*. "It's still hard to identify that this is a fishing rod," she says, referring to a pole with a crank attached to it.

Joselit asks Logan: "The captions have the materials, right?"

"That'll help," Beth says.

"It should say 'fishing rod,'" Joselit adds for emphasis.

Logan explains the next image: "There's a little bit of the room background left behind the sculpture," he says, "which was just me not having the time to do a perfect silhouette. Rachel likes it that way, with the bits of picture left in. I think it's funny.

"And this," he continues, "is a new work."

"A work that Rachel wants to add to the checklist," Gordillo explains.

"Who owns it?" Sussman asks.

"The same collector in Toronto," Gordillo replies.

"Our budgeting department has been doing the specs based on what we had before," Sussman says evenly. "Throwing in a city like Toronto makes everything go—" She finishes the thought with a gesture, lifting her hands off the table as if it were suddenly scorching hot. Logan clicks on, to a stack of boxes.

Next, we're looking at a framed picture of a picture of Marilyn Monroe propped up on a stack of Sheetrock and aluminum studs—Harrison's *Marilyn with Wall*, an ongoing work, in which she relocates the photo each time on a different wall. The questions Harrison's images raise and the need for—or the resolve to do without—more information recur several times more. Harrison prefers to keep interpretations of her work open-ended, resisting any gestures that might be construed as telling people what to think. But while Sussman doesn't disagree with that position, she's also sympathetic to the uninitiated coming to the art cold.

"Just to pause for a minute," she says. "David, do you feel

the viewer is on board or have we reached a state of visual confusion? Do you think a level of clarity is maintained?"

"I think it's a question of how these works are identified," Joselit says. "I don't think it has to be for dummies."

"Rachel is writing some descriptions that will be pretty explanatory," Gordillo adds.

Joselit nods. "Some of these clarifying signals don't have to be her responsibility," he says.

Multiple images of the same sculpture come up on the screen. "This is one that's different from every angle," Joselit notes.

"You've seen this straightforward view of it first," Logan says, assuring the group that viewers have the visual means to get oriented, even if it requires some effort on their part.

"Maybe there could be a list of captions at the end," Gordillo says.

"Not to belabor this," Joselit persists, "because I know Rachel wants to keep things unfixed, but the show will be on the record and we have to be clear."

Sussman stops Logan's progression at a photo of a colorful sculpture in a gallery with what she calls "a yucky-colored floor."

"It's ugly," Joselit agrees.

"And this sculpture is so vivid," Sussman says.

Beth Turk makes the case that this lends the book "a certain honesty: you can't control the conditions of sculpture," she says.

Logan moves on to *Lady Marjorie and Mrs. Bridges*, its title taken from two characters from *Upstairs, Downstairs*, the seventies TV drama. The work consists of a monumental pile of bulging garbage bags inside a loft. First-time viewers of Harrison's work can be forgiven for wondering whether this is sculpture or trash awaiting a move to the curb for pickup.

Sussman readily admits that her first reaction to the work of many of the artists she has championed over the years was one of perplexity. The perplexity drew her in, made her want to learn more. But, I argue, that's probably not true of most of the rest of us. More often than not, perplexity is off-putting, and it drives people away. For those who aren't indoctrinated into the conventions of contemporary art, sculpture like Harrison's garbage bags or even Gober's sinks may create the impression that art speaks to an elitist tribe in a language that the average person doesn't understand. Those who persevere, only to discover that the meaning of the art is in fact up for grabs, may have a low tolerance for ambiguity.

"I love ambiguity," Sussman says. Joselit believes this is the source of her fascination with Harrison. "Rachel's work resists closure," he says, and Sussman is capable of holding two different or even contradictory thoughts simultaneously. Even so, she acknowledges that for many people the concern that they're not coming up with the correct answer takes over; they assume that there's a right interpretation and a wrong one, and nothing in between. Or, Sussman adds, "they think they're on the receiving end of something meant to overwhelm them and show them how stupid they are." Her job, she says, is to help even the most skeptical people find a way into the work via the artist's mind.

But there's no question, she admits, that knowledge of art, like that of antique furniture or wines or opera—fields in which connoisseurship is equated with sophistication—is often wielded as a tool for one-upmanship. Sussman understands because she's been there. "I think we all have the sense that somebody always knows more than we do—that if we don't know that much, it's embarrassing. I mean, believe me, sometimes I go to an artist's studio or somebody's home and there's something hanging on a wall, and someone will say, 'Of course, I don't have to tell you what this is or who it's by.' And I have no idea. And I have to decide: Am I going to reveal to this person that a curator at the Whitney Museum doesn't know the answer? Not only am I unable to come up with something clever or astute, I don't even know the appropriate response that someone in my position ought to have. Believe me, that's happened to me. It's something I've had to get over, too."

## 12

Sussman's commitment to mounting only shows about women artists, though entirely sincere, didn't last. There were men artists, too, who were underappreciated and poorly understood. In addition to Kelley, she brought to the fore Paul Thek, Hélio Oiticica, and Gordon Matta-Clark in individual shows not long after their deaths, presenting their work in all its convoluted originality, for an audience beyond their cohort of admirers. Like Arbus and Hesse, they made work that poses a challenge. Sussman, Rothkopf says, is drawn to artists "who put their finger in the socket of the culture."

Jeffrey Fraenkel says that the artists Sussman takes on, for all their differences, have certain similarities. "A lot of them had troubled lives," he says. "And they're all kind of risky artists to make sense of. All the exhibitions are open-ended. They rarely say, 'This is exactly how it is.' Sussman's approach, as he sees it, "embodies deep respect for the viewer."

"The worst thing you can do is dumb it down," she claims. "If you say it's simple and you make it simple, you've lost it. You've got to defend complexity."

FOR THE THEK (2010) and Oiticica (2017) exhibitions, Sussman collaborated with Lynn Zelevansky, a former curator from the Museum of Modern Art and the Los Angeles County Museum of Art. The shows were shared between the Carnegie Museum of Art, in Pittsburgh, of which Zelvansky was by this time the director, and the Whitney, although each venue gave them a slightly different emphasis. "We were told that you could never do a Thek show or an Oiticica show," Zelevansky recalls. Of Sussman's determination to proceed regardless, she says, "I think she loves the challenge. Besides, you can't just decide after somebody has done this amazing work that you're going to let it die. Somehow we had to figure out a way to show it."

Thek, according to Zelevansky, was "kind of a sleeper"—not off the radar but a bit of an enigma. "Nobody knew very much about him, apart from a few people who had known him personally; and not many people had a sense of the trajectory of his career: what he did and why he did it." Most famous for his meat pieces—wax casts of raw meat or human limbs encased, like reliquaries, in plexiglass vitrines—he lived in New York and died of AIDS at fifty-four, in 1988. Thek was deeply religious; Catholicism is a persistent theme. As it happened, the largest holding of his work was in Germany, at the Kolumba Museum, run by the Archdiocese of Cologne, which over the years had made only occasional small loans of his sculpture. But knowing how much Thek had wanted a retrospective in his own country, the Kolumba agreed to cooperate with Sussman and Zelevansky, sending pieces that hadn't been seen in the U.S. for several decades.

In the cases of both Thek and Oiticica, many of the issues revolved around how to represent works that no longer exist—questions that are "front and center for a whole generation of artists whose work was more conceptual," Zelevansky says. For Thek, for instance, there was often no finished "product" per se. When he was doing installations, he would work every night in the museum; viewers would see a show different from what it had been the day before, much of it made from ephemeral items and materials put together for that moment, most of which didn't survive.

For Oiticica, a Brazilian artist whose best-known work, *Tropicália*, lent its name to a countercultural movement called Tropicalismo, there were large gaps, owing to the fact that a fire had destroyed much of his inventory. In the show at the Carnegie, Zelevansky was content to include reproductions of some of the works that had been lost—a decision that defied standard practice—provided it was clear that they were copies; Sussman, in the show at the Whitney, was not. They used projections to introduce more light; they used videos, then needed to help viewers distinguish between which were documentary and which were the actual art.

As for Matta-Clark, not only was his career remarkably brief, confined to less than a decade, but his works, experienced at the time by a relatively small number of viewers, left behind few if any artifacts. His work can easily come across as impenetrable. Trained as an architect, concerned with urban spaces, social change, and a sense of place, he made interventions—cutting through houses and other buildings—that served as performances, documented in photos and on film. Inevitably the changes he made to the structures left them one step closer to demolition. On a note-card recording his ideas for "Anarchitecture," Matta-Clark wrote:

HERE IS WHAT WE HAVE TO OFFER
YOU IN ITS MOST ELABORATE
FORM—CONFUSION
GUIDED BY A CLEAR SENSE OF PURPOSE

Tony Ganz, whose collection also includes work by Thek and Matta-Clark, says, "You're talking about two of the great artists of the second half of the twentieth century, but until Elisabeth got involved, they were outsider artists. That's a term that means something else now, but I think it's an accurate assessment of what their status used to be. It wasn't that many years ago that you tried to talk to people about Matta-Clark or Thek and, even among curators, they barely knew who they were. Or if they knew, they had limited exposure to the work itself. And that's very different now. In that sense, she has had a real impact on art history."

Sussman takes artists who are, if not unknown, then certainly under-known, "and she mainstreams them," David

Ross says, "registering their work on a museum public."

Uncovering artists who are in some way marginal and bringing them to the center is interesting work, Zelevansky claims, "because not only are you giving the artists credit for what they've done and bringing their work to people that they might not know; you're also playing with the culture—the way the margins and the center interact and sometimes change places."

Spending time with Sussman, you come to realize just how subjective history can be: the extent to which theories about influences, movements, and greatness have been slanted to dwell on some artists and pass over others. In our conversation with Gober, Sussman mentions a recent revival of interest in the work of Alan Turner, an artist she found out about through Gober's Cable Gallery installation back in the eighties. "There are these people who are lost along the way," she says.

Sussman has spent her career extolling the accomplishments of artists relegated to some magnitude of obscurity. Panetta says that teasing out "untold antihero narratives" is something Sussman came to "because that's how her mind works; it wasn't the political issue of the day." Her instincts and the times now seem perfectly aligned.

## 13

America's longstanding love affair with youth—our deeply entrenched assumption that younger is better—has lately found new justification in the digital divide. In cynical terms, Sussman's recruiting Sanders as a partner in 2012 might be interpreted as another case of a dinosaur latching onto someone decades younger as a way of staying current. But, Sanders says, that's not the way he experienced their collaboration. "Elisabeth's not some culture vulture who's just trying to keep up, consuming and recirculating what she sees."

Like fashion and music, contemporary art is always on the lookout for the next big thing—a perpetual hunt that inevitably skews young. "We were reacting thoughtfully to this incessant charge toward 'discovery' and newness as a dominant impetus in biennials," Sanders continues. "For sure, we included emerging artists who really excited us, but we also sensed the deep value in championing artists with long careers who had been overlooked, who were for whatever reasons known more as 'cult' figures, or who were making significant work at a later moment in their career. This exploded sense of relevance, discovery, and emergence came very naturally and felt right to us. Artists were embedding their own investigations of historical, radical artists in their contemporary work: Richard Hawkins embodying Tatsumi Hijikata, the founder of Butoh; Sarah Michelson considering Lucinda Childs and other Judson-era dance practices; Werner Herzog animating etchings by Hercules Segers—just to name a few. I think this anticipated some of the strong rediscovery or revisionist work we see happening throughout the art, music, and performance worlds now."

Adam Weinberg recalls a conversation he had years ago with Martin Friedman, former director of the Walker Art Center, in Minneapolis, and, according to Weinberg, his mentor. He was teasing Friedman, who was thirty years older, about not liking a young artist's work. And Friedman replied, "You, too, will become a victim of your generation." To be a great contemporary curator, one must avoid that fate, Weinberg says.

And, he adds, Sussman has done so. "I would say, by far, the greater number of contemporary curators really have a very hard time stretching much more than one generation—maybe, if they're lucky, two. But Elisabeth approaches art with an innocence of eye, an openness of mind, a curiosity, an empathy, that is so profound that it makes it possible for her to bridge multiple generations."

If she has no sense of time having passed her by, perhaps at least in part it's because the issues that now preoccupy the culture are the ones that have preoccupied her all along. "The ideas that formed me so strongly—Berkeley, the sixties—remain with me," she says. "I'm still strangely attracted to the new. And I retain my interest in the people working at the edges," which, she notes, has become even more valuable in the current climate.

Some things you don't learn in school—not even in all the years it takes to get a doctorate. Recent generations, according to Weinberg, approach the art with a framework of critical theory and history—"all of which is important," he says, "and Elisabeth is very knowledgeable in that regard: she reads a lot, she talks to a lot of people from a lot of different backgrounds." But over and above all that, he continues, is "the understanding of the maker. In the end, what happens in the studio is the relationship between artists and the object or concept or idea that they are trying to realize.

And that's something you can only learn from the inside out, by being with artists."

This is where Sussman's younger colleagues end up learning by proximity, watching her listen, quietly registering the kinds of questions she asks. "I was so inspired by her ability to get under the hood of artists' work," Jay Sanders says. "I learned a lot from her lived experience."

"I sought her out," says Jane Panetta. "I thought, 'Oh, I'm working at the museum at the same time as Elisabeth Sussman, and even though I'm not working *for* her, this feels like a special opportunity.' She has really been a mentor to younger colleagues—to women in particular. Unfortunately, that's less common than it should be in the art world."

Sussman believes in fostering the next generation, according to Sanders. Panetta notes that partnering with colleagues who are younger and greener, as Sussman has done repeatedly, isn't always so easy, requiring explanations and occasional do-overs. "But she's been committed to that. I think she's been a pioneer in terms of bringing junior colleagues into coproducing and co-curating shows. Often the model in the seventies and eighties and nineties was some poor slob of a curatorial assistant in the back room, working for hours, who's probably really smart but invisible labor—never seen and barely mentioned. And I feel like Elisabeth's not comfortable with that from an ethical standpoint."

The list of assistants, collaborators, and others who have benefited from her example and guidance is by this time long and distinguished: David Joselit; Thelma Golden; Elisabeth Sherman, now an assistant curator at the Whitney; Dana Miller, former curator of collections at the Whitney; Tina Kukielski, executive director of Art21; Claire Gilman, curator of The Drawing Center; Kelly Long, her current assistant, whose future she has in mind; and Scott Rothkopf, who, the summer before his senior year of college, assisted Sussman with her Hesse research. "It's funny to go from being someone's intern to being a fellow curator to being her boss," Rothkopf says. "I've learned so much from Elisabeth. But now also to have her support and her wisdom and her moral authority means a lot. The other curators who work here, particularly the young women, really look up to her."

In the Whitney's biweekly curatorial meetings, Jane Panetta says that Sussman "still feels like a very important voice." The agenda's "nuts and bolts," like reviewing gifts and exhibition proposals, can quickly veer off into more macro conversations: "What do we want the program to look like in the next six months or eighteen months? How do we balance prewar interests with contemporary interests? Is there enough gender diversity?" and so on. "And that becomes a way to get to know everyone in this department," Panetta says. Sussman "brings both her knowledge of the Whitney and a continually refreshed take on what we might be doing institutionally."

Panetta consults Sussman not only on curatorial matters but also on career strategy, soliciting her recommendations for negotiating complicated situations. In particular, Panetta admires the decisions Sussman has made in her own life—like how to handle gallery openings, art fairs, dinners, and other seemingly extracurricular events that are nonetheless part of the job. "I decided that insofar as I was going to go beyond the nine-to-five or nine-to-six hours, I would do it on my own and not place those demands on my husband," Sussman explains. "I couldn't ask him to take on the Prince Philip role." As with many artists, it can be hard sometimes to figure out where the work leaves off and the life begins.

Thelma Golden says Sussman "allowed me to understand what leadership could look like for me." One year after the

1993 Biennial, Golden curated a show at the Whitney called *Black Male*, a provocative and thorough examination of the way black men had been viewed in the culture. "Those are probably the two most important shows I'll make in my career," she says, "and they happened early. To be prepared for that professionally, you have to be supported. Elisabeth supported me, not only by making me confront everything I did with rigor and intensity, but also by creating a space in which she allowed me to work through my ideas and ideals with her as a witness and a real co-conspirator toward the goals of that moment. The opportunity to form your path isn't simply a matter of acquiring the skills you need but also to be able to engage in a community of support that allows you to progress."

Sussman's choice to remain a curator rather than climbing the ladder to bigger titles and higher salaries is one that many younger women in the field look to when considering their own options. "As I'm getting older," says Jane Panetta, now forty-six, "people are talking to me about my career path, and I think of Elisabeth, who has taken a stand: she's a curator, and she's not going to feel compromised or like she didn't succeed just because she didn't pursue the job at the top.

"She's this amazing combination: very smart, reasonable, but also kind of fearless. And I think that feels like a good nexus. That's how I want to navigate in the world myself," Panetta adds.

Jay Sanders says, "Elisabeth taught me a certain humble elegance and tenacity, as a way you can live in all this"—the encounters, the dinners, the art fairs. He calls Sussman "the person I would most like to be like."

In Adam Weinberg's telling, Martin Friedman's rejoinder is about the pitfalls of growing old in a field that runs on ideas and aesthetics, which change continually. But surely the dangers in becoming a victim of one's generation aren't confined to old age. Millennials are no less susceptible to this fate than baby boomers. The goal, it would seem—for everyone, of all ages—is to break free of the narrow perspective that sets in among peers, to expand the repertory of the works that inform our thinking to include those that have come before we were born and those that come after the formative years of our youth, and to cultivate an understanding that goes beyond period trappings and allows us to see ourselves on the continuum of what it means to be human.

Among the artists included in the 2012 Biennial was Nick

Mauss, then thirty-two. Sanders, whom Mauss already knew, and Sussman, whom he'd never met, paid him a studio visit that went on for hours. "I've always loved being in dialogue with people of other generations," Mauss says. Curating—incorporating others' work and orchestrating it—is a central component of his art, and the first show he curated, in a room at the Chelsea Hotel, came out of his frustration with the shows he was seeing, all of them for an audience of gallery-goers in their twenties and thirties. He wanted to do something that addressed people of other ages. Not coincidentally, history became part of the subject. In 2012, Mauss re-created a room designed by Christian Bérard for Guerlain in the 1930s and populated it with objects chosen mostly from the Whitney's collection, giving them a new context. Sussman, he says, "drew me out and seemed to be able to follow what I was doing and in some ways understand it better than I did."

After the Biennial, Sussman and Mauss continued their dialogue as his career progressed in the U.S. and in Europe. "She sensed that I was working not as a curator but as an artist using museum objects as my material, and she asked if I'd be interested in doing that with the Whitney's collection, bringing things to light that hadn't been seen or restored, in relationships nobody else would come up with. And that was a step forward for me—something she saw embedded in my work." The result was *Nick Mauss: Transmissions*, a solo show at the Whitney in 2018 that assembled set designs by Eugene Berman, portraits of dancers by George Platt Lynes and Carl Van Vechten, film of George Balanchine's early choreography, Sergei Diaghilev's calling card as it had been displayed in Lincoln Kirstein's house, and other vestiges of the circle surrounding the ballet in New York in the thirties and forties as it continued in its transition to modernism. The galleries, redolent of the stages and studios of the time, served as the setting for live performances by a group of dancers.

Some viewers expressed confusion, wanting to know what Mauss had actually made, apart from presenting sculptures, drawings, photographs, and films by other people. "There were many things that I made," he says, "but to distinguish between them and the rest is something that I feel is not in service of the work." This "disappearing act," in which he recedes into the material—his own and other people's—is in fact part of the intent, "to acknowledge an aspect of my work in process that would not necessarily be visible in the display of things that I made by myself. So behind that was also the idea that tracing lines of influence and constructing a genealogy for my own work is part of the work."

Mauss says that, compared to most curators, Sussman operates according to a different sense of time. "She's capable of this long-range commitment that allows the relationship between the artist and the curator to develop, but also for the work to emerge." In the case of "Transmissions," she became a sounding board and has continued in that capacity for the book that will follow, to which she's contributing an essay. Younger curators Mauss has worked with have been unable to engage and sustain a relationship of this duration. "Maybe it's a matter of where Elisabeth is at this point in her career," he says. Rather than volunteering her knowledge, she reveals things slowly. But over time he has come to appreciate what a panoramic frame of reference she has: "Working with her has helped me formulate myself as an artist and made me a better artist."

## 14

Sussman's success as a curator predates this age of career counseling, with all the personality testing and networking opportunities at our disposal. Her path has not been "linear," to borrow a term often used to describe a direct route to the summit of any given field. In fact, it has been anything but, with occasional detours and other presumed wastes of time. People in their twenties today are encouraged to have a five-year plan; they're told to imagine where they want to be at age forty. Sussman had no plan. Had anyone asked her where she would like to see herself at any point in the future, she would have had no ready answer.

The great virtue of stories like hers is their testimony to the zigzag pattern of our lives, as those of us without a mission that asserts itself early on (to become a doctor, an astronaut, a president) grope toward whatever comes next with nothing more to guide us than our interests. You could argue that Sussman pursued her so-called passion, but the truth is that it took some time to sort out just what that passion might be, and it has continued to change and redefine itself with each new project. So, despite the fact that her story is too idiosyncratic to serve as a road map, it is testimony to how far you can go by putting one foot in front of the other.

Sussman's achievement in retrospect seems both perfectly logical, given her skills, and incredible, because curating contemporary art is a specialty that barely existed when she entered the field. Like most people who know better than to attribute their success entirely to their own efforts and talent, she considers herself lucky. But if, as the saying goes in sports, the harder you practice, the luckier you get, then Sussman's luck improved the more she got to know artists and delved deeper into their work.

In the course of some two dozen interviews with her present and former colleagues, two words kept recurring. One was "innocence," used to refer to her approach, her obliviousness to ulterior agendas; the other was "pure," which is to say that the way she goes about her job hasn't been contaminated by more commercial considerations. Neither of which, everyone hastened to add, is to say that Sussman is naïve. It was her response to the art that got her into doing this in the first place, and it's still the art that compels her.

That quality—what Jeffrey Fraenkel calls being "besotted with art"—is to his mind the most essential factor on which to build a life as a curator. "And I actually don't think that can be acquired or taught," he says. "Either you're besotted with art or you're not."

Assuming for a moment that you are, what can you do to lay the groundwork for a career at the level of excellence that has consistently characterized Sussman's? I asked people in the field. The consensus was that an education in art history is paramount, although there was some disagreement as to whether a doctoral degree is all that necessary these days. "I tend to hire more people who study art history than curatorial studies," Scott Rothkopf explains. "In the last two years, I've hired five curators at this museum, and one has no graduate degree. I hired him because of his relationship to the artists of his time. And then I've hired other people— the print and drawings curator and the director of the collection—who have PhD's, very serious art historians who understand how the institution works. There are thirty-five people on the curatorial staff, if you include assistants, and everyone's got a different role to play."

A number of people I spoke with recommended getting to know as many artists as possible as soon as possible. When

Rothkopf first moved to New York, he became friends with people in their mid- to late twenties who were making art. "And I learned more from them than I did from a lot of my professors in graduate school," he says. He encourages young people to "participate in your moment, in whatever generational sensibility that may be in terms of the music you're listening to and the things you're arguing about."

There was unanimous consensus on the importance of training your eye by familiarizing yourself with great art—a task the internet has made infinitely easier than it used to be. "See as much as you can," Rothkopf says. "Go to as many galleries and museums as you can, read as many art blogs as you can, follow as much art as you can on Instagram. You have to build this expansive image bank in your mind, and looking and canvassing the field is what allows you to start making judgments."

Are some people better positioned to enter the field than others? You might think that geography and early exposure would constitute a head start, but, Jeffrey Fraenkel says, "it's not a matter of being born in New York as the epicenter of the art world or even growing up in a town with a great museum."

David Joselit agrees: you have to start somewhere, he says, wherever you may be. The important thing is to "immerse yourself and do the work, whether that means going to see lots of shows or starting small gallery spaces or writing criticism or making studio visits. Curating is a kind of practice, and I think you have to practice."

The ability to write well is crucial. Seek out a teacher whose feedback contains a low percentage of flattery, who can help you hone your grammar, structure your arguments, and find the most engaging way to tell a story. Learn how to speak in public, to communicate information and ideas.

"As an artist, I have the choice: I can talk about my work or not," Robert Gober observes. "Both things are valid. But as a curator you don't have that option, because you're the interface between the mute object and the public. That was the hardest thing for me about curating: you've got to talk to your board, the committee that's going to give you the funds, the committee that's going to buy something for the collection. Then you've got this group of people coming through, and then you've got kids on a school visit—you're communicating all the time about the art."

As I made a list of the attributes that have propelled Sussman to the top of her field, it occurred to me that they constitute not only a set of skills but also a constellation of character traits, and I think they're worth enumerating, if only to illustrate that being a curator isn't so much a job as a vocation. Among her personal qualifications:

Genuine curiosity, not only about ideas but also about other people. When you interview people for a living, as I do, they turn the tables on occasion, asking where you're from or wanting to hear your opinion—perfunctory questions that temporarily reroute the conversation as a two-way street. Celebrities in particular do this, to such an extent that I assume it's a tactic coached by their publicists; maybe it'll pay off in a more favorable story or at the very least buy them a few minutes' respite from the machine-gun fire of relentless interrogation. Sussman did this, too, although in her case it seemed to come from a different place. Answering my questions, she would periodically redirect the conversation back to me, as if to address some imbalance. What did *my* father do? How had *I* learned to draw? Over a few weeks I came to understand that she was doing this reflexively, having grown tired of talking about herself. Her interest was not a ploy. She wanted to know more about this person quizzing her, as if it weren't fair that I was learning so much about her when she was learning so little about me. In an age of epic narcissism, when people broadcast their achievements, their haircuts, and their lunch, Sussman is more interested in other people's experience than she is in her own.

This is the way she has earned the trust of artists and others who are notoriously skeptical and difficult to deal with: she listens. Not simply taking turns talking, as polite people do in conversation, but registering what the other person is saying, incorporating this new information with what she knows so far, and pausing to ask questions when they arise. She has opinions, which she's willing to offer if asked, although she doesn't lead with them.

"In order to really understand the art from the inside out, you have to give yourself over to the artist's ideas and visions completely," Adam Weinberg says. "Elisabeth is able to do that as a human being. It's a process that requires both empathy and critical faculties, because it's not just that you can empathize. It's also the ability to look at the work in a critical and intellectual way and say, 'What is it that really matters here, and why? What is it that this artist is trying to do that is unlike what any other artist is trying to do? What makes this artist unique?'"

People often credit Sussman with being open-minded, which, as Rothkopf is quick to note, "sounds as though you might like everything," whereas her taste is broad but discriminating. Jane Panetta admires her capacity to change her mind, which she has done on occasion when presented with fresh evidence or a better argument.

Tenacity and patience have stood her in good stead during the long haul often required to make exhibitions happen.

And integrity. "The New York art world's a very clubby place," David Ross says. "It's easy to find yourself all of a sudden in somebody's pocket. In an unregulated art market, with a lot of curators underpaid and overworked, the temptation to play little games and do it in a way that wouldn't be easily discovered is everywhere. Elisabeth never took gifts, never took the summer vacation. She's completely ethical."

While it's true that her personality has served her exceptionally well in her profession, you don't have to be Elisabeth Sussman to be a curator. Still, it wouldn't hurt to emulate her. Many of the character traits that have been crucial to her success are ones that can be developed through practice. Cultivating kindness. Being patient. Looking to see. Taking an active interest in other people. Listening closely. Continuing to look. Persevering when you believe in the project or the cause. Loving words. Learning diplomacy. Looking again. And giving every artist the benefit of the doubt.

# RECOMMENDED READING

For a bird's-eye view, Hans-Ulrich Obrist's *A Brief History of Curating* (Zurich: JRP Ringier, 2009) consists of eleven interviews with veterans he calls "pioneers of curating," including Walter Hopps, Harald Szeemann (one of Sussman's heroes), Anne d'Harnoncourt, and Lucy Lippard. The conversations provide a good sense of the early years as curators of contemporary art invented their own roles in the culture.

Hopps was also profiled in *The New Yorker* by Calvin Tomkins ("A Touch for the Now," July 29, 1991). Charismatic and mercurial, with unpredictable work habits and brilliant insights, Hopps was the founding director of the Menil Collection and a force in contemporary art in California and on the East Coast.

Lynn Zelevansky's superb essay, "Dorothy Miller's 'Americans,' 1942–63" (Elderfield, John, ed. *The Museum of Modern Art at Mid-Century: At Home and Abroad.* Studies in Modern Art, no. 4. New York: Museum of Modern Art,

1994) revisits the series of exhibitions that Miller mounted and situates her career as a woman at a time when and an institution where masculine values prevailed.

*Diane Arbus: A Chronology* (Aperture, 2011) is a just-the-facts chronicle pieced together from notebooks, interviews, letters, appointment books, postcards, and other fragmentary evidence of Arbus's everyday life, assembled by Sussman and Doon Arbus. This first appeared as an extended section of *Diane Arbus Revelations* (Random House, 2003), the catalog for the Arbus retrospective Sussman mounted at the San Francisco Museum of Modern Art.

*Diane Arbus: Untitled* (New York: Aperture, 1995), originally published some twenty-five years prior to this latest exhibition at the David Zwirner Gallery in New York in 2018, doesn't contain the full complement of the sixty-six images Doon Arbus selected as the definitive version of her mother's final project, but those that are included convey the profoundly moving nature of the work, along with Doon's elegiac essay.

In *Silent Dialogues: Diane Arbus & Howard Nemerov* (San Francisco: Fraenkel Gallery, 2015), Alexander Nemerov does a parallel reading of his father's poetry and his aunt's photography and the many ways their preoccupations intertwined, mining what feels like a lifetime's worth of reflection.

*Robert Gober: The Heart Is Not a Metaphor* (New York: Museum of Modern Art, 2014) does for Gober what Sussman's Chronology did for Arbus, furnishing the world of ideas and events in which Gober has produced his work, providing context.

Catalogs of Sussman's two Eva Hesse shows—*Eva Hesse* (San Francisco: San Francisco Museum of Modern Art, 2002) for the big retrospective, and *Eva Hesse: Sculpture* (New Haven: Yale University Press, 2006) for the subsequent show at the Jewish Museum in New York—are indispensable to understanding the artist and her work.

*1993 Biennial Exhibition* (New York: Harry N. Abrams, 1993), the catalog for the controversial show Sussman curated along with Thelma Golden, John Hanhardt, and Lisa Phillips, cannot re-create the experience of the art in the galleries, but it's worthwhile for the essays (including Sussman's "Coming Together in Parts: Positive Power in the Art of the Nineties"), which provide a firsthand account of the currents roiling the culture at the time. Of the extensive reconsiderations of the show two decades later, several articles give a good account of where we were and how we got here, most notably: "How Identity Politics Conquered the Art World: An Oral History" by Jerry Saltz and Rachel Corbett (*New York* magazine, April 18, 2016) and "Jerry Saltz on '93 in Art" (*New York* magazine, February 3, 2013). Jennifer Krasinski's "A Brief History of the Whitney Biennial" (*Village Voice*, March 15, 2017) is an excellent guide to the perpetually beleaguered show's history.

Sussman's essays on the artists whose work she has shown are models of how to talk about art without boxing it in, dispensing relevant information so that readers and viewers can arrive at their own interpretations. In particular, see: "The Problem of the Primal Scene," her essay on Robert Gober's installation at Boston's Institute of Contemporary Art, in *Utopia Post Utopia: Configurations of Nature and Culture in Recent Sculpture and Photography* (Boston: MIT Press, 1988); "The Mind Is Vast and Ever Present," in *Gordon Matta-Clark: You Are the Measure* (New York: Whitney Museum of American Art, 2007); "Photography in Life and Death: Paul Thek and Photography," in *Paul Thek: Diver, a Retrospective* (New York: Whitney Museum of American Art, 2010); and her introduction to *Mike Kelley: Catholic Tastes* (New York: Whitney Museum of American Art, 1993).

# ACKNOWLEDGMENTS

Writing is a passport to adventures that lie beyond the lives we've made. I'm grateful to Jonathan Karp, who created the Masters at Work series, for this extended voyage in the art world, and to Stuart Roberts, my editor, who steered me through the process with infinite patience and a steady hand. More thanks to: David Chesanow as copy editor, for the care and precision he brought to the text; Samantha Hoback, production editor, for keeping us all on track; Celeste Phillips, legal consultant, for her close reading and recommendations; and Elise Ringo and Kelly Sullivan, marketer and publicist, respectively, for helping this book find its way into the hands of its audience.

My research brought me into contact with a number of people I'd long admired and others I'm delighted to have met.

For her thoughtful, unstinting cooperation, I'm indebted to Elisabeth Sussman and to her colleagues at the Whitney, who so generously obliged my requests for interviews, reporting, and further information: Adam Weinberg, Director; Scott Rothkopf, Chief Curator; Jane Panetta, Associate Curator; Kelly Long, Curatorial Assistant; and Stephen Soba, Director of Communications.

Ted Bonin, Helen Charash, Jeffrey Fraenkel, Tony Ganz, Sondra Gilman, Robert Gober, Thelma Golden, David Joselit, Nick Mauss, David Ross, Jay Sanders, and Lynn Zelevansky shared insights and recollections that enabled me to see Sussman more three-dimensionally. Elizabeth Easton kindly provided background on the genesis of the Center for Curatorial Leadership, which she founded. I thank them all for their time and those conversations.

As ever, David Kuhn and Nate Muscato, my agents at Aevitas Creative Management, have overseen the contract and finances with efficiency and understanding.

A few friends—Richard Armstrong, Terry Winters, Rob Wynne—provided invaluable reconnaissance at the start and along the way.

My ongoing gratitude goes out to a number of people whose contributions are inconspicuous and unofficial, for tending the home fires during my protracted absences and helping me manage the business of everyday life, enabling me to clear the space and time needed to write: Janise and Keith Loell, Margie and Tom Strayer, Kim Kasper, Joe Stevens, Hollis Hames and Scott Astorino.

And, finally, comprehensive thanks to John Macfarlane, my corner man.

## ABOUT THE AUTHOR

Holly Brubach writes about art, dance, fashion, and other forms of culture. She is a former staff writer at *The New Yorker* and *The Atlantic* and the former style editor at *The New York Times Magazine*. Her work has appeared in *The Gentlewoman*, *W* magazine, *Vanity Fair*, *Architectural Digest*, and many other publications. She is the author of *A Dedicated Follower of Fashion* and *Girlfriend: Men, Women, and Drag*. She is currently working on a biography of ballerina Tanaquil Le Clercq. She lives in Pittsburgh, Pennsylvania.